WISDOM SPEAKS

A Personal Interview™

VOLUME I

Elder Johnnie D. Bond, Sr.

www.TrueVinePublishing.org

Wisdom Speaks: A Personal Interview
Johnnie D. Bond, Sr.

Published by The 24 Minute Ministry™

Book Production by
True Vine Publishing Company
P.O. Box 22448
Nashville, TN 37202
www.TrueVinePublishing.org

ISBN: 978-1-956469-07-3 Paperback
ISBN: 978-1-956469-10-3 Hardback
ISBN: 978-1-956469-08-0 eBook

Copyright © 2021 by Johnnie D. Bond, Sr.
All rights reserved. No part of this book may be reproduced in any form or by any electronic or mechanical means, including information storage and retrieval systems, without permission in writing from the publisher, except by a reviewer who may quote brief passages in review.

Unless otherwise noted, scripture quotations have been taken from the holy Bible, King James Version

Printed in The United States of America—First Printing

FOREWORD

Reading this book has taught me, in its instructions from the Wisdom interviews, that all the hosts of heaven are unified. Their unity is centered around the one called "The Father" and His power is unlimited. He is a life-giving creator. His powers prove His sovereignty. His will and His choice is the same type of will and choice that He gives to all creatures in His image and likeness. He chose to make one creature who pleased Him, His equal without fear of Him practicing ungodliness which would be so contrary to His spiritual nature which is filled with love.

I learned that not one angelic being has ever experienced one ounce of pain. Yet, the one called "The Son of the Highest," a single being of the Father's creation, chose to suffer in pain, humiliation, and at the hands of those much more inferior to His glorious stature and power. He came down from heaven to demonstrate his Father's type of love to a blindfolded society.

Though Jesus was never deterred, He focused on the love relationship He had with His Father to avoid distraction. He listened intently to His Father's instructions and saw step-by-step writings of prophecies that were written by prophets of old. So, He confirmed these delayed and meticulous prophecies and many became a reality during His walk on earth.

This single creature, who is called Jesus, fulfilled these prophecies as His disciples personally witnessed Him on His journey in the land, called Earth, or the Father's battleground.

He was sent to complete the final work and pleasure of His Father. His punishment to be offered up in death. He was buried, then rose up leaving the Earth after He was resurrected from the grave and ascended to the throne of His Father where He awaits in the patience of the Father to cease. Even now, God extends His mercy to the world, before Jesus is sent to Earth again to render justice and judgment on the wicked and rebellious clan of evildoers.

This book is a must-read.

Mrs. M. Bocknite

TABLE OF CONTENTS

Preface 1

My Vision 5

Interviews

Interview One: Possessed from the Beginning 12

Interview Two: Heaven Produces Greatness 20

Interview Three: The Voice from Heaven 26

Interview Four: Who are the Sons Of God? 35

Interview Five: What is Faith? 47

Interview Six: Be Fruitful and Multiply 55

Interview Seven: The Holy Ghost 59

Simple Chats

Chat 1: The Judges 81

Chat 2: Women 87

Chat 3: The Children 93

--Selfie

-- Loved one

A Blessed Family 105

Conclusion 108

Donate To Free Book Campaign 111

Preface

Dear Reader,

Over the years I have found the following scriptures inspiring and they have helped me fulfill my destiny:

"Blessed be the God and Father of our Lord Jesus Christ, who has blessed [me] with all spiritual blessings in Heavenly places in Christ." (Ephesians 1:3).

For to one is given by the Spirit the word of wisdom; to another the word of knowledge by the same Spirit;1 Corinthians 12:8

To now be endowed with the word of Wisdom. I want everyone who will read, listen, and judge for yourselves from my Wisdom's personal interviews; what can be observed in many scriptures; had escaped or had been quiescent In my understanding. Sitting in plain view. Yet, hidden from the wise of this world.

Unlike, what many think, that Wisdom is, an Idea, or a Knowing, my series is going to show you, with biblical references, that Wisdom is way more than that.

She Is knowable,

She gives instructions,

She speaks out,

She laughs,

She is fruitful

She pours out of Her Spirit

She turns a deaf ear to those who refuse Her

She protects from evil!

And more!

Wisdom has been here from the beginning, unveiling a fear, power, and reverence of God's existence. Proverbs 8;22-23.

According to the Holy words, Wisdom identifies as Female, as a mother teaching and instructing our little human minds.

We are little minds in the eyes of the All-knowing creator.

"For as the heavens are higher than the earth, so are my ways higher than your ways and my thoughts [higher] than your thoughts." Isaiah 55:9

Wisdom instructs us in the Fathers ways [today] just as she did for Solomon, as evident in his writings. She shows us the right path. That our feet do not slip.

She is a disciplinarian.

She instructs us to walk on the right path. As you read, you will see that

Wisdom has many spiritual traits to help guide new babes in the faith to maturity by every straight path.

In this series of conversations with wisdom, I ask questions and She responds through scripture.

To give you a glimpse of what is in her right and left hand, of how the Lord gives us His wisdom.

As she describes the events important to the Father's role in destroying the works of the arch-enemy of Christ, the Only Begotten. You will also better understand Her role in the life of the Father's creation.

In this "interview," She answers difficult life's questions all answers from the scriptures.

She also addresses real instances of humanity's greatest woes and the troubled characters

First of all, I never imagined that God would use me to teach his people how to apply their hearts unto wisdom.

However,1Timothy 1:15, I believe Paul's confession perfectly describes at times my faint-hearted demeanor, that Christ came to save sinners, and I am a chief sinner, here I also obtained mercy, through His suffering.

When we add Matthew 23:34," I sent unto you prophets and wise men and teachers..." Jesus here justifies my authority.

Secondly,I never thought that God would use me, again, to teach His people how to number their days through His seven (7) day creation blueprint.

His footprint starts in His creation and they continue to make an impression in the life of every soul through eternity,

To acknowledge and embrace this initial structure promotes harmony with

Him, and with every mortal soul.

All essential for peace and preservation.

Make no mistake, accordingly, the Wisdom from above is first pure, then peaceable, gentle, and easy to be intreated, full

of mercy, good fruits, without partiality, and without hypocrisy.

James 3:17

Study these eight (8) traits again and again carefully, to know true wisdom.

In contrast, the wisdom of this world is foolishness with God...and will allow anyone to gain the world and lose his/her soul. (Mark 8:36),(1Cor.3:19) Prefer the Wisdom from above!

If you have read this far, it means that you too are joining me in this life-changing journey. As She feeds us from Her bosom. Welcome Aboard!!

MY VISION

Hello, I am Elder Johnnie D. Bond, Sr, and this is my book, Wisdom Speaks Volume I

I have learned so much from this personal interview. As the Interviewer, you would not believe how much my faith has been strengthened. These crystal clear revelations will overwhelm you.

Seriously, I had been the person who compared my understanding of the word of God with others.

Not understanding, there is a "mark for the prize of a higher calling of God In Christ Jesus "(Phil 3:17.

Most of our teaching comes from men (pastors),who have formed opinions that if you know more than they know, they would look up one day and that member would have half of his congregation starting a new church down the street. So, they are cautious in ways that limit expansive study in the things of God.

In the following pages, I will teach from the Instructions of Wisdom gleaned in these personal Interviews.

Sharing these instructions will come as enlightening to you as they have been to me.

These proverbial saying leaps off the pages to help us to be more diligent in our search, adding to our faith virtue, and to virtue knowledge and to knowledge self-control. {2 Peter 1:6)

In other words, there is no longer any need for fretting, and being

apprehensive about your standing with Jesus Christ.

Wisdom Speaks, but only a few hear. She calls out in the street, but the god of this world has blinded the eyes of many(Proverbs 8)

In preparation to be a true servant for the Father. For me, it all begin with Alexander Scourby, a global voice that narrated the Old and New Testament for the American Foundation for the Blind. His voice inspired millions of people countless times; off the charts; is an adequate description of his professional prowess.

The Father created Scourby's voice for this purpose to read His Holy words to mankind. Through Scourby, the Father helped millions of people that could not read or write and with difficulty understanding His scripture.

Scourby makes the Bible handy and easy -read Scourby's voice will be a witness against the slothful and wicked who will not adhere to his voice expounding the Holy scriptures...

Therefore, they will not enter the joy of the Lord.

Counter-wise

As I lay comfortably in my bed or sit in my vehicle, my CD player blasts a visual conversation between me and what Scourby reads from the scriptures, that according to Christ, these scriptures are the bread of life, the bread from heaven, flowing like a river of living water into my ears, into my mind, heart, and strengthening my soul to satisfy the seat of my affections, a love for God.

Making truly, the joy of the Lord my strength. (Nehemiah 8:10)

Initially, this practice for me started at age 21 when I heard a preacher from His pulpit say Jesus Christ is the answer. He repeated it three (3) times before it began to make sense to me. I begin to think if Jesus is the the answer, I can get all my answers to my questions by learning more about

Him. A dilemma for me occurred, whenever I picked up my bible to study, I fell

asleep quickly, not even fresh into the text.

Looking back, I can credit the Lord for those heavy eyelids.

Because it pushed me to look for a remedy. That's when Alexander Scourby came to my rescue.

In 1973, a few weeks into my search for answers I purchased Alexander Scourby's Bible version of the New and Old Testament cassette tapes. From then on, I have listened to his readings with attention and clarity over 48 years, especially on long drives serving my customers in nearby cities.

Consuming and digesting these priceless words as valuable nuggets creates precious ornaments about my head.

Now at 69, I perceive to have gained clear knowledge and pearls of wisdom about the uncut and uncensored word of faith.

It's true. A wise man will hear and Increase Learning. Proverbs 1:5

The prolonged activity of hearing the word of God perfected in me, can now perfectly describe my work of faith. Like a fruit tree, the sap, the fluid that circulates within the phloem of a tree

that produces its fruits. The excess of hearing God's Word,

His tactical plans, out of the righteous ways of God has made me a more finished product than when I started the journey.

Now you will witness this transformation in our acts and actions going forward. My spiritual overflow and understanding have started and are now pushing me forward to simply Bless His People. Seriously, you are going to Be Blessed!!!

Now, let me share with you a prime example, over time as I continuously listened, a notable scripture stood

out, It reads, "So teach us to number our days that we may apply our hearts unto wisdom". Psalm 90:12

This scripture begins ringing into my hearing with a special meaning. Akin to approaching a dazzling glaring light, only it was my heightened consciousness being awakened every time I heard the scripture. Mentally, I began to rejoice when the voice of Alexander Scourby approached passages of other scriptures before reciting this verse.

As I dug deeper, the Lord revealed to me [this] scripture is an Answered Prayer Request, But Ironically. No One Knows It?

This revelation came to me in the month Juneteenth became a national holiday. The Lord said to me. Just as the slaves did not know they had been freed. My people do not know this Psalm 90:12 is an Answered Prayer Request. All believers can know how to number their days, and apply their hearts unto wisdom. Wisdom is the principal thing; therefore get wisdom and with all thy getting get understanding.

With both these actions functioning together my people could be benefiting from the freedom it brings...If they can understand. They shall know the truth and this truth shall make them free'er.(St John 8:32)

More insight will be gained from my interviews and will we teach millions now how one should number their days and how they can apply their hearts unto wisdom. "The people that do know their God shall be strong, and do great exploits" (Daniel 11:32) As you read carefully from the Wisdom's comments to the Interviewer, you will see Wisdom taking a spiritual wrecking ball to unbelief and ignorance. As these truths will positively impact your life. You will be amazed and thrilled.

Here is how she begins to demolish disbelief and ignorance. She inspired (3)books, two (2) websites, and an App. When fully functional to then see how the formulas cycle year's table advise you of what to expect in every year of your life as you see the patterns for yourself and in others, you will be thrilled.

This Wisdom Speaks Volume I, mount the barriers against spiritual offenses. Jesus said offences will come attacking aggressively daily.

"For I heard a loud voice saying in heaven, Now is come salvation, and strength, and the kingdom of

God and the power of his Christ for the Accuser; of our brethren are cast down, which accused them before Our God day and night" Revelation 12:10. Most think those evil, lustful impressions in their thoughts are their own. But when they understand Wisdom's instructions that there are evil spiritual frequencies that are picked up in human receptors. If entertained one can become a servant of Sin, and when it is finished death is its wages. So, you didn't think you had a master; an evil master?

Here is Jesus' answer "Whosoever committeth sin is the "servant of sin". Next, He tells you what will happen to anyone, "that servant will not remain in the house of God forever(he gets thrown out on his head) But the Son who is his bouncer will Kick him out. (paraphrased) (St John 8:34-35)"

Wisdom will teach you how to avoid these mental traps, for to number your days one is never confused and can remain focused and motivated. Taking one's cue from the seven (7) days of the Father's creation simply means you acknowledge His control and primer presence in our life.

Don't be simple; if the Seventh (7) day positively affects one's life.

Why wouldn't the other six(6) days contribute to your well-being?

We cannot help those who want to remain ignorant. Want more proof? See His initial guidance for his Host of angelic beings in the start of a new universe in His comment "Let Us" denotes He designates authority, even now on earth this authority is extended to humans that He made giving them the authority to subdue all principality and powers, because, we are complete in Jesus, which is the head of all principality and, power. (Col. 2:10)

All of God's work turned out Good. In His 6 days. I can see "High Fivin" in celebrations as God saw everything that he had made, and behold, it was [Very Good] (Gen.1:31) Call it a conversion, transformation of a void landscape He brought life to be celebrated as a life we all now enjoy. The creation story captures it all. See Genesis 1:1-31 and Genesis 2:1-3

Jesus makes it personal. "If He, The Father so clothed the grass and the lilies of the field How much more shall He also provide and teach anyone with a desire, how to prosper"?(Matt 6:30)

As the Interviewer and Author. At the onset, I know there are three groups my book series will never reach:

1) The simple ones that love simplicity.

2) The scorners who delight in their scorning.

3) The fools who hate knowledge.

To avoid being part of one in any of the three groups: Adopt Wisdom's traits from the scripture above, the eight (8) attributes, to understand true wisdom from Him. Then you must make every effort to understand His seven (7) Formula Cycle Years, and how they establish a foundation for your life,and why they are germane to personal success and to our exegetical text.

Now let's begin my interview with Wisdom set on the stage of Biblical history...Let's discover why the psalmist's request is Answered. From this series, You will also learn how to number your days and why you must apply your heart to wisdom.

As a human, I will be Interviewing Wisdom recording her comments in a series of books and articles. If you've never studied the wisdom communications of the proverbs. My personal interview with Her will certainly increase your understanding of her role in this vast universe called Heaven and Earth.

As I probe Her with these questions, we will get answers straight from Her Lips.

INTERVIEW ONE
POSSESSED FROM THE BEGINNING

Interviewer: Wisdom, thank you for joining me today and everyday. I believe your delight is with the sons of men by your presence with me today. This is astounding and breathtaking for men to have access to unrestricted Wisdom.

Wisdom: Yes, initiating a conversation that started ages ago, when the Lord possessed me at the beginning of His way. And it's now great to be in discussions in your series.

Interviewer: To be called on by our Lord. This statement is profound. Was this joyful for you?

Wisdom: I agree this statement *is* profound. I rejoice in the habitable part of His earth, by your human exploration we know not all parts are habitable. My delights were and are yet with the sons of men.

Interviewer: My studies reveal you were established from everlasting, from the beginning, or ever the Earth was.

Wisdom: Yes, to my delight, one of the sons of men is my Lord, your Savior Jesus, who was declared as a greater man of wisdom than Solomon." Matt 12:42. Amazing right! Yet, you ask most religious leaders today who was the wisest man in the Bible; they will say, Solomon. WRONG ANSWER!!! "The LORD possessed me in the beginning of His way, from his works of old. To assist in the foundation of this whole earth Proverbs." 8:22-31.

Interviewer: Wisdom, explain further, what do you mean when you say, "He possessed me at the beginning of his way?"

Wisdom: Son, imagine you are in the ubiquitous presence of the Father. All Life springs from His throne of glory, creating souls, creatures called Angels. As His love continuously overflows, you'd never want to experience anything outside it; because outside His love is the opposite of His Love.

Take the angelic character, Lucifer, who fell from grace. Jesus discussed a fellow spiritual authority who had breached a command, "Moreover, if thy brother shall trespass against you, go to tell him his fault between you and him alone: if he shall hear you, have gained a brother." As the Son explains, when action is offensive, the trespasser should be approached alone, in a respectful manner, so he is comfortable receiving corrections. If he receives those corrections, you've gained a brother. Matthew 18:15-17.

As you know, the Son loves righteousness, hates iniquities, and leads by example. So after recognizing the sin, and because sin is an abomination to Father's law, Jesus approached Lucifer. But the fellow, Lucifer, would not hear, so He brought me, Wisdom, onto the scene. The fellow would not listen to Us, so then He brought Lucifer to our heavenly-host council, and Lucifer still would not listen. Failure provoked his sin for Sin is the abomination of the Father"s Law. So, as the Son said, I saw Satan as lightning falling from Heaven; I witnessed his fall. In other words, Satan got kicked out of Heaven with all the followers of his order, meaning they were all guilty of the same sin and rebellion that Lucifer had committed.

Interviewer: This sounds like the beginning of rebellion.

Wisdom: Yes! The Father got involved. He told the Son in Psalms 110:1, 'Sit here as I make the enemy your footstool." I witnessed Lucifer's fall; but before, he had an honorable role, Son of the Morning, with a glorious spiritual countenance. But now, he is banished and counted as a condemned heathen. This was the beginning of the "Law of Sin and Death," a total separation, and absence from the Father's love, approval, and presence. Before this, nothing so perverse had ever been exposed in the Father's dwelling.

Interviewer: So before this horrible disorder, the throne room of God was a kingdom of perfection?

Wisdom: Yes! We, those in heaven, have this phrase, "You're dead to me." The phrase applies to your spirits as well as your body of humanity. Anyone the Lord judges to receive this spiritual death penalty will be separated from God's Omnipresence to suffer in unquenchable fires with burning brimstones for all eternity.

We were ordered to begin digging a pit for those banished, for you creatures, humans, who refuse Christ's redemption will also occupy at the Father's appointed time.

Interviewer: YIPES! I recall David said, "Let their table be a snare, a trap, a stumbling block and a recompense unto them."

Wisdom: Even though God removed Lucifer from Heaven, and the banishment was justified; a case had to be proven with witnesses, God would have to satisfy Mercy and Judgment. I got to witness the type of galaxy He needed for the judicial courts and battlefield. The Father's choice is Earth, a dark void and desolate hemisphere. It was all water-filled with nothing, no life. No appearance of life existed anywhere.

As the Father's angelic hosts appeared on the scene, His Spirit moved upon the face of the waters. He requested light and divided it from the darkness, naming them both. He made the firmament to be divided and created a space between the water above and beneath. The upper firmament He called Heaven, and so it was named Heaven and that day ended. "And God said, let there be a firmament in the midst of the waters, and let it divide the waters from the waters." Genesis 1:6. We, the heavenly hosts, still only had water.

The evening and the morning would create a new day. Then the Father said, "Let the waters under the heavens be gathered together into one place, and let what we knew to be a matter of some kind. He called it dry land or earth, then He pooled together all the water in one place and called it Seas. And God said, let the waters under the heavens be gathered together unto one place, and let the dry land appear: and it was so. And God called the dry land Earth; and the gathering together of the waters and He called them seas: and God saw that it was good." Genesis 1:9-10.

We (namely, Wisdom, Knowledge, and Jesus) continued the activity of the proposed creation. With the Son being the chief appointed over the Father's house and who had possessed me from the beginning of His way. We moved forward, with additional works of the new creation.

Interviewer: What a task at hand and it seems you were all working in harmony?

Wisdom: Yes! The evening and the morning created a new day, so the Father said, "Let the earth bring forth grass, then we made a botanical garden stretching for miles and miles east, west, north, south in the vast open space under the heavens." And He said, "Let the earth bring forth grass, the herb yielding seed, and the fruit tree yielding fruit after his kind, whose seed is in itself, upon the earth: and it was so." Genesis 1:11.

Interviewer: So, you're saying that if the Father did not speak anything on this day, the Earth would have been a barren geographic surface, like the moon, or other galaxies in His universe with no water or provisions to sustain life as I enjoy today? Nothing would grow?

Wisdom: Correct. As you can observe, the Father is making improvements each day that follows the last. The evening and the morning created a new day. To distinguish the night from the day required two lights, a greater and a lesser light, which also denoted signs and seasons. "And God said, let there be lights in the firmament of heaven to divide the day from the night, and let them be for signs, and for seasons, and for days, and years. And let them be for lights in the firmament of the heaven to give light upon the earth: and it was so. And God made two great lights; the greater light to rule the day, and the lesser light to rule the night, and he made the stars also. And God set them in the firmament of heaven to give light upon the earth, and to rule over the day and over the night, and to divide the light from the darkness: and God saw that it was good." Genesis 1:14-18.

Interviewer: So to get our days and years, He allows the greater and lesser lights, stars to give allumination upon the earth, and the evening and the morning creates a new day?

Wisdom: Yes! You witness this day in and day out, year after year. Meanwhile, another improvement is waiting in the wings (no pun intended about his angels). The Father said, "Let the waters bring forth abundantly the moving creature that hath life, and the fowls that may fly above the earth in the open firmament of heaven. And God created great whales, and every living creature that moved, which the waters brought forth abundantly, after their kind, and every winged fowl after his kind; and God saw that it was good. And God blessed them, saying, 'Be fruitful, and multiply, and fill the waters in the seas, and let fowl multiply in the earth.'" Genesis 1:20-22.

Wisdom pauses.

Interviewers: Please continue; this is fascinating.

Wisdom: Son, everything thus far the Father had approved. We were all excited that we had pleased the Father. Even the beast of the fields. All cattle, creeping things, bugs, flies, lice, and ticks, have been approved. I believe He said that it was good. The evening and the morning created a new day. So far, every day came with its changes and I must say, they were marvelously breathtaking.

So, it's day six and this next day wasn't left aside. All the angels were waiting in anticipation, desiring to see what the Father would do on this day.

You see, the earth's matter was inferior to our composition. Our life springs from His Spirit and His desire for unique and powerful creatures.

My son, in the beginning, (using here Moses's account) on this sixth day the Son called me forward to gather various specialists for this upcoming task. So, I assembled those in their restricted fields, to work with the dust of the earth, to create a living Soul to have the same image and likeness of the Son.

The new creature was called "Man," a creation from the dust of the earth. The Father further extracted from his rib to give him his counterpart, whom He called "Woman." He blessed them, and gave them the first command; to be fruitful to replenish the earth, bearing seed of their kind.

Interviewer: Again, I am awed by your coordinating efforts of the team of the angelic hosts who followed all your instructions.

Wisdom: Then the Father gave humanity authority over all the other creatures. And God blessed them, and God said unto them, "Be fruitful, and multiply, and replenish the earth, and subdue it: and have dominion over the fish of the sea, and over the fowl of the air, and over every living thing that moveth upon the earth.' And God said, 'Behold, I have given you every herb bearing seed, which is upon the face of all the earth, and every tree, in the which is the fruit of a tree yielding seed; to you it shall be for meat.'" Genesis 1:28-29.

At this point, the Father rested.

Interviewer: Well yeah, who wouldn't need a rest after all that?

Wisdom: It's not that he needed rest but that it would set a precedent to his creation: Rest for the land in certain seasons, rest for man on his journey, and an acknowledgment that one day a week should be observed as Holy unto the Father's Awesomeness. He then made our Lord the Lord of this Day.

INTERVIEW TWO
HEAVEN PRODUCES GREATNESS

Interviewer: Who is greatest in the kingdom of heaven?

Wisdom: Great question. The disciples asked Jesus the same, "Who is greatest in the kingdom of heaven?" Matt.18:1. To answer this question, Jesus did not think like a mere man. He spoke from a position of the Heavenly, the divine ideal for all creatures. Just like the angels, who have enormous potential bestowed upon them, still respond only in obedience; so Christ here with a child admonishes His disciples.

You see a single angel has the ability in strength to dive deep into the earth and shoulder the greatest of mountains, heaving them toward the widest of seas. An angel can smite a nation and do the supernatural, but they only act under authority, displaying humility in all instances. They can solve the most complicated equations conceived by mankind in the blink of an eye. And they have the capacity to heal, and can heal the worst of sickness only on command. Some angels can cause prosperity in a wasteland, and others can restore favor for the repulsive, but only on command.

Whatever the task, the Father knows which angel He created to accomplish it. There's even an angel to number every hair on a man's head. But in every case, they act only as directed by the Creator.

Interviewer: Wow, specific angels for specific tasks... Cool!

Wisdom: Yes! God created His angels and bestowed them with their varied capabilities and they answer only to Him. So noted Jesus from birth to his cross, He gave his angels charge concerning Christ. Of a truth, they were to bear him up at any time lest he dashed his foot against a stone on any occasion. Psalms 91:11-12.

Jesus knows that this child-like submission is the ideal state. Little wonder, He demonstrated this to three (3) of his disciples at the mountain top where they experienced his origin through transfiguration. Then charged them to tell no man until after His resurrection. "For I came down from heaven, not to do my own will, but the will of Him that sent me." St John 6:38

Wisdom: Son, do you notice the consistency? Even Jesus was not about his own will, but the Father's will.

Interviewer: Yeah. A great thing about maintaining this posture is that we can recognize our inadequacies as children to do so, then we're not claiming perfection as adults.

Wisdom: There is too much in the vastness of this universe, made by an infinite God, to absorb in a glance. The know-it-all's don't Know It All. "And if any man thinks that he knows anything, he knoweth nothing yet as he ought to know." 1 Corinthians 8:2.

All Apostles, especially Paul and John understood that Satan's constant manipulation in the affairs of men would require them to be led as children by the Spirit of God, to remain Sons of God. Remember, the angels only respond when they are summoned. Because of their reverent fear and love of the Father, all their abilities and gifts are harnessed and humbled to only his commands as that of a child to a parent.

Consider this scripture, "Yet Michael the archangel, when contending with the devil, he disputed about the body of Moses, durst not bring against him a railing accusation, but said 'The Lord rebuke thee.'" Jude 1:9.

Interviewer: Was the demonstration here humility or obedience?

Wisdom: Both. For a moment, take your eyes off the Angel, and to the Father. Even in a serious situation explained by Jude, the Father did not command harm or destruction of Satan before his time. Instead, he said to Michael the ArchAngel, "Take up Moses' body and do no harm."

Interviewer: I think most humans would have taken revenge, or harmed him, when he refused the body of Moses, provoking a war among nations.

Wisdom: Yes! But even the demeanor of one of the most powerful holy angels, Michael, cared about only one thing, respect for all the Father's creatures and commands.

Think about that!

All of you are of one flesh, brothers and sisters, and His creatures as well. So you must love each other as you love yourself, God's second command. Denoting love cannot make a distinction, it is just love. Even Christ admonishes us to love our enemies. Matt. 5:44.

"The LORD hath made all things for himself: yea, even the wicked for the day of evil..." Proverbs 16:4. This is a true statement. The pit we dug for the devil and his angels will soon be their eternal torturing home. Please warn others that they should not have a desire to join him. Such humility in man is a must-have. It is a license. Otherwise, they will not enter the kingdom in heaven.

By this, you will know the throne of the Father is REAL, void of chaos and corruption. Never again will a criminal enterprise start up or occupy the place of the Father's Throne Room. My son, let His love be your priority. Jesus shows the humility of his Father's angels always beholding His face in contrast with a child gazing up to a parent for guidance.

Jesus teaches that one must possess this type of submissiveness to enter the kingdom of heaven. It is *love* personified, not fear; this is an endearment to our Maker. The angelic hosts witness this awesomeness daily. As weaker vessels in the presence of the enemy, humans are smothered by Lucifer, the prince of the powers of this world, with temptations; the same temptations that were offered to Jesus in his wilderness experience. Matt 4:1-11. Few learn how to resist his temptations. Remember Christ's prayer for you? "Lead us not into temptation, but deliver us from evil" Matt.6:13.

Interviewer: Oh yeah, I know that prayer well.

Wisdom: The major prerequisite to occupy the kingdom of heaven is to be BORN AGAIN,

to first

*See it.

*Acknowledge it,

*Value it, then

*Enter it. Doing so you will be

*Delivered from death, hell, and the grave.

(S.A.V.E.D).

Son as a born-again, if someone says to you- you are too spiritual that's the point of being born again. One is transformed from the carnal mind to that of the spiritual mind. Observe these Wisdom Nuggets:

"Be transformed by the renewing of the mind"

"Occupy a seat in heavenly places in Christ Jesus"

"Set your affections on things above and not on things on the Earth"

"Don't accept their mockery, continue to pursue a stature and fullness of your Lord"

Elder Johnnie D. Bond, Sr.

"Let this mind be in you that is also in Christ Jesus"

My son, one must absorb my instructions, possess the right way daily, and maintain a hunger for righteousness.

Interviewer: All these Wisdom Nuggets will be on my journey to spiritual maturity.

Wisdom: Here are the final examples my Son: Jesus says, "Except ye be converted, and become as little children, ye shall not enter the kingdom of heaven." Matt 18:3. And the humble act of Mary sitting, listening, having a continuous hunger and thirst for the righteousness that proceeds in and from the Holy scripture. Luke 10:41.

My son, I, Wisdom, dwell with Prudence, and find knowledge of witty inventions. Proverbs 8:12). We pass these instructions on to the meek in the human race. It's not the singer or artist's talent, it's our instructions. Not the skill of any creature but those who will follow my instructions. Knowing this truth, begets the motivation for the Father's artists and writers to provide inspiration that adds to your secret closet worship experience daily.

Solomon preferred me over fame and riches, to his credit the Father gave him both. There are many other examples that speak to the greatest in the kingdom. One of the disciples could have just raised a mirror to the face of our Lord and saw Him (the GREATEST).

INTERVIEW THREE
THE VOICE FROM HEAVEN

Interviewer: Can you explain the Voice from heaven that came as a fearful sound according to Peter, James, and John.

Wisdom Speaks: Son, allow me to give you context regarding this scene. By human scientist's estimation, the earth is 4.543 billion years old. That would mean someone created this body of land and water and made it fruitful, and habitable that long ago or sometime between then and now. This plant world provides provisions for Anthropomorphics and Animalia. If I use the scientist's estimation for a relationship between the two parties, the Father and Jesus, His Son, has had a relationship for a very long time, "And now, O Father, glorify me with thine own self with the glory which I had with you before the world was." St. John 17:5.

Imagine! How long this period was!

Interviewer: My mind can scarcely grasp the fruit yielded by such a long relationship.

Wisdom: Just wait, I have a lot to say about relationships. The following scene and Voice speak to this relationship. "And the Lord said, 'Shall I hide from Abraham that thing which I do?'" Genesis 18:17.

The law of Moses established that two or more witnesses were required to judge or complete any task of judgment. The Father had commanded it to be carried out. The angels approached Abraham later to be identified as Christ acknowledged this protocol in the Sodom and Gomorrah incident. "Abraham rejoiced to see my day and was glad" St John 8:56…..Abraham prepared a meal for the strangers and a relationship established, sparking a discussion by Christ and Abraham of sparing the cities, though unfruitful. Only Abraham's nephew Lot and his 2 daughters were spared escaping destruction of wicked towns.

Interviewer: This taught me that I can negotiate with my Lord!

Wisdom: Exactly. Do you remember how Abraham started his negotiations to save the cities, requesting that only ten righteousness be found to spare them? His 10 numbers were not found.

The Lord said Because the cry of Sodom and Gomorrah is great, and because their sin is very grievous, He has to render judgment on these cities.

The Voice from Heaven

Here we see another relationship cemented, and Abraham would become a blessing to all nations through his children.

Interviewer: I can only dream of leaving such a heritage for my children.

Wisdom: Son, the three (3), were chosen to witness the voice from Heaven on the mountain top. The scenery is unique. It articulates that after six (6) days Jesus took with him Peter, James, and John. These three (3) and their early experiences with Christ are equivalent to some of your comedic characters known as The Three Stooges.

Interviewer: Because they kept making errors in judgment? Or falling down and accidentally hurting each other?

Wisdom: Sort of. These disciples did not want children to come to Christ, attempted to refuse blind men from speaking loudly to get Christ's attention, and complained that the pricey ointment used for Christ's burial and earthly departure should have been sold and profits used to feed the poor.

Jesus rebuked that suggestion and declared a memorial to acknowledge the woman who anointed his body for burial with the expensive ointment, that she would always be remembered as his Gospel message is preached to all the world.

Yet, even though Peter, James, and John characterized the Biblical Three Stooges, Christ wanted them to witness this scene so they could further understand His sacred mission to ordain the Father's wishes that they may understand their own greatness and role to further the Father's Redemption Goals.

Elder Johnnie D. Bond, Sr.

At this scene Elijah and Moses were summoned. Beforehand, as great leaders, they were those whose bodies never saw a grave but were caught up in chariots of fire. Jesus's brief glowing appearance revealed His relationship to Moses and Elijah as they governed His chosen people and journeyed toward redemption for mankind in the era of their time on earth.

Interviewer: Riiiiight. I am impressed. As a son of man the Lord's closeness to his disciples, Moses and Elijah, Jesus here demonstrates how deep any man's relationship could be with Him.

Wisdom: Yes, you're getting it! Remember, "And beginning at Moses and all the prophets, He expounded unto them in all the scriptures the things concerning Himself." Luke 24:27.

In Jesus's lifetime on earth, Jews would question the relationship of that as God being hIs Father. St John 5:18. Making Himself equal to God was punishable by stoning. Christ's voyage on Earth, and even to this day, would not change all non-believers into believers. Jesus acknowledged this when he described those Jews questioning him by saying they were not legitimate seeds of Abraham if they refused Him. He declared they were of their father, the devil, who was a liar and murderer from the beginning, and abode not in the truth. When he (Satan) speaks a lie, he speaks of himself as he is a liar and the Father of lying. St John 8:39-45. He follows with the statement, "If I say I do not know the Father I would be a liar like unto you: but I know him, and keep His saying." St John 8:55.

In another relationship, John the Baptist bears witness that Jesus was before him; that Jesus was the lamb. That he (John) came to make straight the way of the Lord, that he (John) would

The Voice from Heaven

decrease as Christ would Increase, coming before Jesus. John declared he attempted to straighten the path before his appearance. St John 1:23. And, "Prepare you the way of the Lord and make his path straight." Isaiah 40:3

Christ's authority was heavily scrutinized. Although many in the public had received Him. The leaders of the time - who should have known Jesus - offered himself as a lamb to be slaughtered for the sins of the people. Many described Jesus negatively. Although He requested that He be judged by the works of miracles He performed on thousands and by these acts they should have believed in Him. But also did His brothers believe in Him. St John 7:5.

When they saw him casting out devils. They judged that he could only do so by Beelzebub, a prince of devils. They called him a glutton, a winebibber, who ate and drank with publicans and sinners, and rejected him.

But let's go back to this scene on the mountain, Christ is transfigured before three (3) disciples Peter, James, and John. His face appears as bright sun, His garments are as white as the light. Afterwards, He would charge them to tell no man. But instead of enjoying the moment, Peter has a bright idea. But as Peter expressed his bright idea, he provoked the righteous indignation of the Father. That's when angels and I, Wisdom, hovered over them with a bright cloud shadowing them, in your vernacular. We spread a red carpet for the Father's appearance as He spoke this powerful truth. The truth that Christ is the Son of God and that all should hear Him should be ringing around the world even now.

Elder Johnnie D. Bond, Sr.

Son, the message in God's voice has a zealous tone that serves His affirmation and confirmation. *"This is my beloved Son in whom I am well-pleased* **Hear Him**,*"* this message is ignored today in your leaders' pulpits. One of your famous actors said to his director, "I don't care what movie you put me in, *just make me the star*" (Gary Cooper). This blasting trumpet sound from the player's embouchure, is to be made by every preacher about Jesus.

Listen to Me, **Wisdom**. All Preachers, going forward, every message that you preach should *"MAKE JESUS THE STAR". "MAKE JESUS THE STAR!"* He is the savior, the **Bright and Morning Star**, and the lover of your souls. Do you want your land healed? Jesus is the answer. Do you want your sins forgiven? Jesus is the answer. Do you want peace on Earth? Jesus is the answer. The number of people who have already died from God's plague (Covid) has already exceeded the numbers that died in the age-old Flood waters. And you have not addressed the seriousness of it! And you have not addressed the spiritual significance of it. *And you think God will relent of His anger?*

Interviewer interrupts: Wait a minute Wisdom, the statement you just made is a call to action as we speak in this very interview.

Wisdom continues: Yes. This statement, *"This is my beloved Son in whom I am well-pleased* **Hear Him**,*"* is akin to your phrase, "A Shot heard around the world!" This statement must be shared and quoted in every temple, synagogue, and church building, forever, until He comes. This is the personal acknowledgment of the relationship created in the beginning. For, in the beginning was the Word, and the Word was with God and the Word was

God and the Word became flesh from the dust of the earth. (St John 1:1) This flesh was made of lesser matter than the angels. His Son took on flesh, He made himself of no reputation, and took upon Him the form of a servant and was made in the likeness of men. And being found in fashion as a man, he humbled himself, and became obedient unto death, even the death of the cross. (Philippians 2:7-8) His resurrection created a new creature, a Quickening Spirit, for a new house; "Now you are Christ's house if you hold fast to the end of a time only known to the Father." (Hebrews 3:6.)

Son, there are thousands of instructions I have to give, but only those who acknowledge God the Father's statement will understand my instructions. As I have said, the simple ones love simplicity and fools hate my knowledge, but *you* can inspire new relationships by reviving these words, "**This is my beloved Son in whom I am well pleased.**"

Interviewer: I say I hear you Lord, help me accomplish this work to the end,. feed me til I want no more. Then feed me more.

Wisdom: Hear! Listen! In Christ's own words applicable today, are messages in disgust and anger toward leadership who have seized His vineyard on earth to possess it only for personal gains:

"But woe unto you, scribes and Pharisees, hypocrites! for ye shut up the kingdom of heaven against men: for ye neither go in yourselves, neither suffer ye them that are entering to go in. Woe unto you, scribes and Pharisees, hypocrites! for ye devour widows' houses, and for a pretense make long prayer: therefore ye shall receive the greater damnation. Woe unto you, scribes and Pharisees, hypocrites! for ye compass sea and land to make one proselyte, and when he is made, ye make him twofold more the child of hell than yourselves.

Elder Johnnie D. Bond, Sr.

Woe unto you, ye blind guides, which say, Whosoever shall swear by the temple, it is nothing; but whosoever shall swear by the gold of the temple, he is a debtor! Ye fools and blind: for whether is greater, the gold, or the temple that sanctifieth the gold? And, Whosoever shall swear by the altar, it is nothing; but whosoever sweareth by the gift that is upon it, he is guilty. Ye fools and blind: for whether is greater, the gift, or the altar that sanctifieth the gift? Whoso therefore shall swear by the altar, sweareth by it, and by all things thereon. And whoso shall swear by the temple, sweareth by it, and by him that dwelleth therein. And he that shall swear by heaven, sweareth by the throne of God, and by him that sitteth thereon. Woe unto you, scribes and Pharisees, hypocrites! For ye pay tithe of mint and anise and cumin, and have omitted the weightier matters of the law, judgment, mercy, and faith: these ought ye to have done, and not to leave the other undone.

Ye blind guides, which strain at a gnat, and swallow a camel. Woe unto you, scribes and Pharisees, hypocrites! for ye make clean the outside of the cup and of the platter, but within they are full of extortion and excess. Thou blind Pharisee, cleanse first that which is within the cup and platter, that the outside of them may be clean also. Woe unto you, scribes and Pharisees, hypocrites! for ye are like unto whited sepulchers, which indeed appear beautiful outward, but are within full of dead men's bones, and of all uncleanness. Even so ye also outwardly appear righteous unto men, but within ye are full of hypocrisy and iniquity.

Woe unto you, scribes and Pharisees, hypocrites! Because ye build the tombs of the prophets, and garnish the sepulchers of the righteous, and say, If we had been in the days of our fathers, we would not have been partakers with them in the blood of the prophets. Wherefore ye be witnesses unto yourselves, that ye are the children of them which killed the prophets. Fill ye up then the measure of your fathers. Ye serpents, ye generation of vipers, how can ye escape the damnation of hell? Wherefore, behold, I send unto you prophets, and wise men, and scribes: and some of them ye shall kill and

The Voice from Heaven

crucify; and some of them shall ye scourge in your synagogues, and persecute them from city to city. That upon you may come all the righteous blood shed upon the earth, from the blood of righteous Abel unto the blood of Zacharias son of Barachias, whom ye slew between the temple and the altar. Verily I say unto you, All these things shall come upon this generation. O Jerusalem, Jerusalem, thou that killest the prophets, and stonest them which are sent unto thee, how often would I have gathered thy children together, even as a hen gathereth her chickens under her wings, and ye would not! Behold, your house is left unto you desolate. For I say unto you, Ye shall not see me henceforth, till ye shall say, Blessed is he that cometh in the name of the Lord." Matt 23:13-39.

Interviewer: Whoa. The text above indicates that Christ didn't need twisted cords to beat upon these leaders, the Pharisees and the like. If one updates these leadership titles to Bishops, Evangelists, and Elders, then Jesus would be very grieved also with them today.

Wisdom: The Voice from heaven came to leave no doubt about the **Relationship** between the Father and His Beloved Son, who He sacrificed for the sins of the Whole World.

INTERVIEW FOUR
WHO ARE THE SONS OF GOD?

Interviewer: Can you clarify who the Sons of God are in the scriptures?

Wisdom: John puts it simply in 1:12, "For as many as received Him to them gave He power to become the Sons of God." Son, listen to a mother, as this is often a rejoicing salutation from any mother, it's written Gen 4:1, "And Adam knew Eve, his wife, and she conceived, and bare Cain." She was excited and said, "I have gotten a man from the Lord." Not, I offer this man-child to the Lord, but he is *mine*.

I would love to point out this as the origin of thought behind Paul's instructions to Timothy to the church. During the time of this writing, most didn't have firsthand knowledge of the words of Jesus. Apostle Paul felt that women would supersede and teach their children the ways of their idols, since that was all most of them knew. That teaching would jeopardize all the effort he had put into teaching them about the grace and salvation made available to them through faith in Christ Jesus. So, he said, "I forbid a woman to teach or have too much authority in the church. A woman who does not completely understand nor will abide by God's strict teachings cannot raise a child in the fear and admonition of the Lord." 1 Timothy 2:12-14.

Interviewer: Yeah, women weren't allowed to have leadership positions in the church for a long time because of these words.

Wisdom: Paul pointed out the level of moral decadence that is caused by a lack of true instruction in righteousness which resulted in a wreck of too many societies. In a more poignant point I will explain. But to continue with my thought, Solomon also admonished his sons to get the wisdom early.

He exclaimed that the fear of the Lord is the beginning of my attributes, instructions and knowledge. It is the duty of the parents first to teach their child/children what the fear of the Lord is. With the advances in interpretation and access to the written word of God today, along with the plethora of teachers in your society, could enable Paul to revise his commentary, but it is what is in print in your bible in this 21 century era.

Interviewer: Concerning sons of God; what do you think was the Father's intention when He breathed the breath of life into Adam's nostrils thereby creating a living soul? Would he be a Son of God?

Wisdom: God created this new creature, first with the ability to learn, then earn Sonship Status through inheritance when Christ became the Son of Man.

From the beginning of this earthly created creature's existence, From him (Adam) He would create a Spiritual Quickening Man. A Son of Man. A Life-Giver. A Conqueror of the Rebellious, represented and known to us as Jesus, with a name above every name, His only Begotten Son.

My delight alone with more gifts of the Holy Ghost, was with humans, instructing, teaching them to immediately begin to instruct each other in the ways of The Father. From rules already established in the kingdom of heaven. Additionally, we helped name every creature and identify all herbs and plants. The ones that are good for food, medicines, and coverings respectively. The bright shining sun required coverings to be replaced daily, but Adam and Eve enjoyed the fresh plants as comfortable garments. Then the Lord God made them coats of skin to clothe them.

Interviewer: So when God made Adam and Eve there was no community, your priority then was to acclimate them to their environment and establish how a moral society should communicate and thrive in the presence of their creator.

Wisdom: You got it!! All of the laws and rules of heaven had already been established from the beginning, the things that made heaven this non-corrupt kingdom. A moral society should coexist with its Maker. And before a mass population was available to govern, we were there to instruct accordingly to the ways of heaven, to establish on Earth as it is in Heaven. Not the opposite.

Who are the Sons of God?

My son, we were minute by minute on the scene advancing the new creation of the Father. Yet, you will see how the spirit of deception also is on the scene and able to manipulate Eve into disobedience, by eating the forbidden fruit and sharing it with Adam.

Son, you now have a better comprehensive understanding of the perils of living in an environment where failure to heed to a single command of God caused anxiety, disruption, disarray not just to Eve, but to the entirety of creation. The deceiver's influence on that disobedient action cursed the serpent and sent Adam out of the garden of paradise, Eden.

Interviewer: And as a child I onced thought Satan would relent of his evil ways. I see this law of sin mutating from Lucifer's domain to the earthly populace.

Wisdom: Yes, after the Father's verdict, our authority did not change. We continued to see to it that the purpose of the Father was fulfilled. We continued to assist humans with the activity of all seed-bearing, as the command to be fruitful and multiply continued to be the Law in effect.

Eve remembered the curse that humans would eat bread by the sweat of their brow, and that they must till the soil to survive; she raised Cain and taught him planting and harvesting, and how to produce greater and greater harvests year after year. She always showered him with flattering words and shared her pride in his accomplishments.

Meanwhile, the next son, Abel, did not share Cain's enthusiasm about farming. Instead, he was interested in the beast of the fields. In particular, he enjoyed the sheep, the humble and the most vulnerable, the mothers and their little ones who needed even more care after birth.

Cain continued producing greater crops from the rich soil of the earth while Abel tended his great herds. Abel also was receptive to the stories from the Lord God; you may remember the Lord came walking in the cool of the day when He approached Adam hiding, as Adam had discovered he and his wife were naked. The Lord was upright, able to talk with Adam eye to eye, face to face. Abel is taught by the Lord stories concerning the existence of the new living soul, humanity, and their purpose so-designed by the Father. These stories explained why creatures multiply year by year, as their seed continues to reproduce themselves.

Abel learned these stories, later told by Moses during his 40 days in the mountain wilderness after escaping the Egyptian bondage. Abel had been taught why man was formed in the likeness of the Son and His initial purpose.

Son, please note that cultivating tomatoes, beans, and other crops is entirely different than interacting with the beast of the fields; it requires different skill-sets to tame and command the beast of the fields. Tending to these animals, allowed humans to function in their roles to subdue and conquer all in their surroundings. Abel also learned about the Lamb of God who would be subdued, how he surrendered, and how he became a sacrifice for the initial breach in the Father's Kingdom.

Abel also learned that even though the Father felt true love for His Son, Jesus, He sacrificed him, proving that sin will not go unpunished. It worked, the one sacrificed effect, proved the Father's love He has for all in his vast kingdoms; He will kill anyone if they break the least of his commands. The beauty and glory of this is that Jesus was blameless, without blemish, without sin or faults. We all join in to say "Holy, Holy, Holy, to the Lamb of God."

Interviewer: Can I add my salutation now?

Wisdom: It may take too long, let's continue. Abel understood his role while Cain was often concerned about the next great crop. At the end of the harvest season, the two men would bring their best offering to the Lord God as an act of worship and thanksgiving. To show appreciation for the Father's love and care for their existence in His newly created Earth; we observe through our worship also, and humans are required to do the same.

One day, Cain gathered from his vegetation the best of many fruits, seeds, and crops to offer to the Lord. He showed that his offspring would be well-nourished from the earth's land produce. But Abel understood the story of a Lamb's sacrifice and the significant impact it would have for eternal existence for all in God's new creation.

Thus, Abel slayed a lamb, a creature humbly yielding without a mumble, which he brought forward. And he didn't just bring any lamb, he presented the first without blemish, the finest as offering. He did it as a sign of humility, and to show the Father that if sacrifices in life are a requirement, he would sacrifice this creature to Him.

The Lord God was pleased. Upon presentation, The LORD had more respect for Abel's sacrifice than Cain's. Genesis 4:4. As the two men were in the field discussing the matter, Cain saw that slaying something would remove it from existing on the earth. No such action had been performed with a human. Cain saw that destroying an object rids him of that object (or person); he would not have to be a second choice for the Lord God's approval going forward. When the Lord appeared to Cain and He asked, "Where is thy brother?" We cringed at Cain's response. The Lord God said he could hear Abel's blood cry from the earth. Genesis 4:10. Therefore, Cain had not eliminated all traces of Abel; Abel's blood spoke from the earth from whence he came.

My son, here is the first death on earth, but it's not Abel's departure from Earth, it's this statement, "Cain went OUT from the presence of the Lord God." Genesis 4:16. To go out from the presence of God is death, when permanently separated from the love and presence of a living God, you are Dead to Him and all His bountiful blessings.

Interviewer: Is the Law of Sin and Death at Cain's doorstep? Would this be a type of emptiness?

Wisdom: Yes. It also means that one is now in league with the originator of this state of anarchy and lawlessness. Except one repent, turn back into the broken relationship. You are no longer a candidate or in a position to obtain the status Son of God. Remember who was thrust out as quickly as lightning?

Interviewer: Yes, until he is conquered the sting of death belongs to Lucifer. I am beginning to see the reality of God's masterful plan.

Wisdom: Am pleased of your insight of what is to come. Now Adam's next son, a like-kind-seed Seth, would take Abel's place as the one with interest for the ways of the Lord God. So,

Adam and his wife gave birth to a son they called Seth which means Appointed or a Chosen. Genesis. 4:25

Cain cannot possibly be a Son of God anymore; he is in the land of Nod, a place of wandering. Abel no longer exists. The newborn Seth becomes the potential Son of God receiving my instructions; to reproduce the seed of his kind after his likeness. So Seth picks up the traditions of Abel, with my Godly Wisdom, Knowledge and Understanding, to instruct his generations.

Interviewer: Of course thoroughbred horses breed seeds of like-kind. My simple comparison.

Wisdom: Good choice. All through the scriptures prophets are referring to My people. Here is a great analysis, "He came unto his own and his own received him not." St John 1:11. Lastly, Jesus sent out the disciples armed with powers to cast out devils, heal the sick, but only to the house of Israel, the lost sheep of the house of Israel.(Luke 9:1.

We make this distinction because a Separation, a Dividing of Sheep and Goats will be a reality upon Jesus' return.

Interviewer: I understand. It says He will cast out with the devil and his angels. Matt 25:41, Rev 12:7-17.

Wisdom: A Son of God, by Biblical doctrine and instruction, one can reproduce a God-kind of seed, the seed of righteousness; He sows into the things taught to him, proceedings from his innermost being. A seed/word that is Spirit and Life produce the like-kind. The highest form of learning and retention is expressed in the phrase from Christ's statement "eating my flesh and drinking my blood…"it is a suggestion of ingesting all of himself. St John 6:54. This is a spiritual process.

If it is said that the word becomes flesh, then the word can be consumed, ingested, and digested. This action, as with all actions, affects human thought which affects the human spirit. This can transform the metaphorical DNA of anyone to a spiritual formation and produce the like-kind seed. Fruit as from a specific fruit Vine.

It starts in the mind, that if you are an avid student of a particular artist, author, or poet, you will become a product of their tutelage, edification, and training. Paul urged, in Romans 12:2, to be transformed by renewing the mind, and I would further say to be transformed with sound wisdom. Do this with your teacher's ongoing pedagogy, with the Holy Ghost as the first in the lineup of teachers. This will cause anyone to be a carbon copy of His teachers, and to be furnished rightly in the taste of your teacher. To become a branch from an original Vine, to produce seed from the order of that Vine planted by a Husbandman of truth, whom the Father is. It's well-pleasing to that husbandman.

Interviewer: So once one becomes a son, one is always a son?

Wisdom: My son please understand clearly what am about to say. If a person chooses at any point to be unbelieving, simple, or unlearned, Jesus let you know that they will not earn a Sonship status. A change of heart because the Lord's coming is delayed, or begins to fight, eat, and drink with the drunken, or he is unaware of the time, he is cut asunder, he is appointed as a hypocrite and cast into outer darkness. Matt 24:48-51.

Christ's authority grants this power to become a Son of God as a virtue of a believer's willingness to learn and be transformed by the instructions of the Holy Ghost. I am a Gift here also to assist. We will deliver by keeping believers on a straight path. The Holy Ghost is the Spirit of Truth. You cannot get lied to or deceived. We create the greatness in you, a phenomenal creature, to counter the he that is in the world. A deceiver who accuses you daily of the Father. The thoughts of lust, greed, anger without a cause are all evil frequencies.

Believers must resist them, with whatever things are true, honest, just, pure, lovely, true, of good report, seasoned with virtue and praise. Thinking only on these things.(Phil 4:8.Keeping the eyes on Jesus the author and finisher of their Faith.

Failure for us is not an option. The fault will never lie at our feet.

As long as anyone fails to yield to all of our instructions they will remain a simple one; essentially, they will be no different from sinners. Many think that if they are unaware of certain facts, they will not be held accountable. My son, unbelievers are going to hell with the hypocrites.

Interviewer: Now I understand why one cannot always be a Son. **It's tragic** for those who take the same route of Cain to go out from the Lord.

Wisdom: Let's now begin with our instructions to Seth, who attained sonship status and taught his generations the ethics and precepts of the ways of the Lord God.

Enoch, the seventh from Adam, was an excellent example of Seth's offspring, an honored student. He became a prophet and a preacher of righteousness saying, "The Lord God would come with many thousands of his saints to render judgment on the whole world." Jude 1:14.

This prophecy is still outstanding. We await for His trumpet sound which will be glorious to some and a dreadful sound to others. Enoch walked with and pleased the Lord so much that God took him and didn't allow him to taste death as you know It.

My son Genesis 6 began the rehearsal prophecy to Enoch's prophecy, the flood waters. The Lord's first judgment on an entire society is another reason Paul warned of teaching by people, man or woman without godly understanding. It states, "When men began to multiply on the face of the earth and daughters were born unto them, that the sons of God (those of Seth lineage) saw the daughters of men (those of Cain's Lineage) that these daughters were fair (beautiful) the Sons of God took them wives of all which they chose.

Observe this scripture, "And God saw that the wickedness of man was great in the earth and that every imagination of the thoughts of his heart was only evil continually." Genesis 6:5. Mixed marriages were not the issue here, failure to meditate, embrace the Law of the Spirit of life in the perseverance of Life went silent. (Crickets!!)

Your lesson here, raising your offspring in the fear and admonition of the ways of God, teaches your offspring the sacredness of God's way. To have done so during this generation of humanity may have avoided condemning this human race to death in a 40 day and night flood on the earth.

Who are the Sons of God?

Interviewer: So, proving here again that God will not tolerate a criminal enterprise very long?

Wisdom: Correct. We have said God is Love. This will always be true. But to help you understand better, note:

Your United States is a democracy for good, but judges are appointed to lock your ASS UP (not referring to a Jackass) when you break the settled Laws. Sometimes there's mercy but often there's no compromising, and if a person is found guilty of committing a cold blooded murder, based on your law, one could FRY. Remember, it repented the Lord that he had made man and grieved him and us all to our hearts (Genesis 6:6). And also remember Jesus did not give the order to wipe out all of this society. Only the Father possessed that authority, by which only eight souls were saved from the destructive floodwaters. Can you count the number of children that died in the womb?

Beloved, now are we the sons of God, and it doth not yet appear what we shall be: but we know that, when He shall appear, we shall be like Him; for we shall see Him as He Is. And every man that has this hope in Him, By his words, will keep himself pure as Jesus is Pure." I John 3:2.

INTERVIEW FIVE
WHAT IS FAITH?

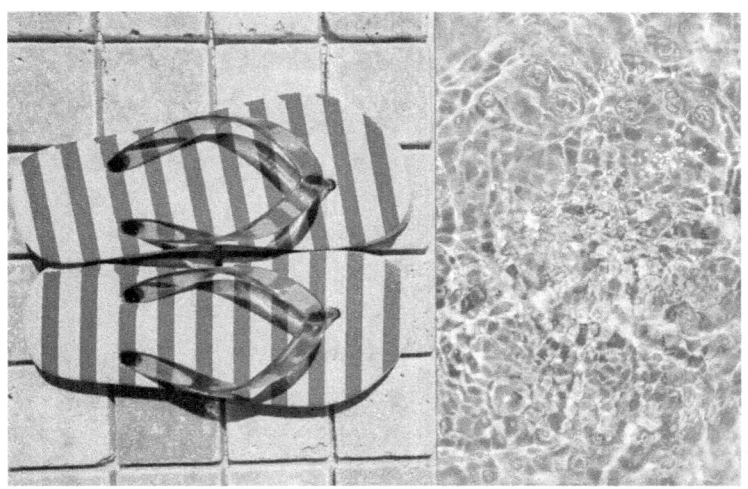

Missing feet. Faith must be walking on water.

Interviewer: What is your understanding of Faith?

Wisdom: My son, Christ always tied *faith* to what you should understand about the organization, functions and operations in heaven. He desired that "on Earth as it is in heaven" will be the standard and reality of how earthlings performed, not the other way around. The conduct in heaven is how true societal conduct should be on Earth.

No one commits adultery, there is no criminal enterprise in heaven. There are no schemes to gain power, fame, and money, or riches, or stealing, or bearing false witness against a neighbor

What is Faith?

in heaven, no race wars or claims of territory dominance. Yes, God's love allows a perfect society to exist because there is no scarcity, or the like, of sharing with others in heaven. Lucifer wanted more power than was afforded him. He actually thought he could obtain this power by amassing more followers. A simple statement flew over his head that he missed, "The Father rejects the proud but He gives grace to the humble." James 4:6.

In Matthew 17:19 the disciples ask Jesus, "Why could we not cast out demons in the lunatic son brought to us by his father? Jesus answered, pointing to their faith. Oh, ye of little faith."

Contrast this scene with the centurion soldier in Matt 8:8-13. The soldier acknowledged that where Christ came from, heaven, Jesus could grant His authority to suffice everywhere. Christ didn't have to be at the specific place to get things done. All that was needed was His word. Hear what Christ said about the Roman Centurion, "He turned to the crowd and said, 'I have not found so great FAITH, no, not in Israel.'" Matt 8:10.

Interviewer: If only we could govern our society as it is in heaven, without the interference of the wicked voice of Lucifer's regime, that would be profound.

Wisdom: True. But here, no one in all of Israel, except John the Baptist and the Centurion Soldier, had been able to associate Jesus with His spiritual authority. The Jewish People wanted an earthly king to overthrow the oppressors ruling that day. My son, here is the faith Christ always wants!

- An understanding that He came down from heaven where greater forces exist.

- An understanding that unless believers speak in the authority of Him, devils will not recognize men's wishes.

- An understanding that the Father shows him all things, and has committed all judgment unto Him, because he is a peer of men.

- An understanding that the Holy Ghost is now presently, here, on Earth, dwelling in Christ followers, responsible for communicating, and promoting the Father's will to lift up Jesus, his Son, to save all that will call on Him.

We leave intact the Father's true identity. GOD IS LOVE! (1 John 4:8) But Jesus is your judge. The Father has committed all judgment to the Son because He is the son of man. St John 5:22. You guys get judged by a peer, Jesus, not an angel, but the one liken unto yourselves. GOD IS LOVE! Thus, Jesus said, "And if I judge, my judgment is righteous judgment." St. John 7:24. Having been given the power to cast out devils and cure disease, in previous instances, His disciples did not attempt to say, "In Jesus' name I command you devils, to come out of this son." Luke 9:1. So Christ scolded them calling them a faithless and perverse generation. Matt 17:17.

They should have known from all his previous acts, that he was (and is) the greatest spiritual force that can subjugate inferior forces to himself. That their lives should be to walk in his authority and not in a carnal state of mind. Then their faith would allow them to move mountains, or curse barren fig trees at the root of their existence. But, now, Jesus said they had little faith.

Jesus further acknowledged that along with faith the kind of evil forces that had occupied this son required a greater focus

What is Faith?

than what only Fasting could produce. Fasting rids your mind, body, and senses of irritability. Giving the Faster increased spiritual awareness and control. They can see outside their personal surroundings to see into a spiritual realm. You could say that you are seeing where, how, and why those evil spirits inhabit the body. Why were they taking up their space in their victim in the first place?

Interviewer: I can attest that when I fast I am more focused and in control. Fasting works for me, as you have stated. But I'll leave the demon-casting to Christ.

Wisdom: In another instance, Jesus describes what happens when the unclean spirits are gone out of that vessel and seeks to return. Matt 12:43. If the delivered person has not filled the space, the evil spirit will return with higher ranking demons and the next state of the person will be worse than the first.

Jesus often said, "Go your way, sin no more lest a worse thing come upon you." John 5:14. He is saying to all, "Abide in my word, my presence, to become stronger in the innerman. His words help to accomplish this. Know that Lucifer prowls as a roaring lion moving about seeking whom he may devour. Resist the devil and he will flee from you." 1 Peter 5:9.

Interviewer: Thanks for the clarity. Now I can remain even more focused to refuse old wives fables, and exercise myself rather unto godliness, for godliness is profitable unto all things. (1 Timothy 4:7)

Wisdom: My son, out of the real context, many people incorrectly quote Paul's Hebrews. Faith is... scripture. It's like saying, "Now is time to eat." The author Paul says that from all that I said to you in this epistle, let this spiritual substance which are my words create hopefulness within you with no physical evidence, just my words. Let them be your Faith. Take your belief out of Earth's spiritual world and realms and go into the heavenly.

Whatever you see in the physical, first started in the spiritual. Sometimes it is important to take your eyes off the physical to stop looking for physical evidence. One will never have a true love for the kingdom of God while loving the world or the things of the world. (1 John 2:15) Set your affections on things above. Seek those things that are above where Christ sits at the right hand of Power.

My son, orders from heaven are the origin of *faith*. To believe is the act, based on heavenly orders, and are examples for your faith. Only believe! Jesus said to one father; with tears the Father replied Lord, "I believe; help thou my unbelief." (Mark 9:24) With tears, they are legal when an urgent matter determines life or death, health, and well-being. When you believe that He is, and that He rewards those that diligently seek him, that is Faith. (Hebrews 11:6)

When you understand the inheritance of the meek, humility, the examples explained in a previous conversation your faith can take you into heavenly places. Knowing you may be in that posture for a time, there to remain as long as it takes:

- to *hear,*

- *to obtain wisdom,*

- *there to observe,*

- *there to meditate,*

What is Faith?

- to be comforted within. Faith is your substance.

Your faith, if you hold it, rejoice in it, praise God for it, He will not despise you for it. A broken and contrite heart is not despised.

Interviewer: Are you saying the physical appearance should be ignored to have a perfect faith?

Wisdom: My son, Phillip said to Jesus show us the Father, then we will be satisfied. (St John 14:8) Jesus said to him, "Have I been with you so long, and yet you have not known Me, Philip? He who has seen Me has seen the Father; so how can you say, 'Show us the Father'? (St John 14:8-9) Son, in these scripture and thereafter replace the word "believest" with "Faith in me". That's how one faith should react. A holy-spirit being can dwell within a body. Christ previously defined the Father as "God is a Spirit;" He can occupy anything, anytime, anywhere, and within a physical character to instruct them in the person of himself.

Look at the contrast. Then entered Satan into Judas. (Luke 22:3) This occupation was brief. Yet it was complete to accomplish the betrayal of Christ. If you continue inflexible, relentless, steadfast in Jesus' teaching, the Apostle's doctrine, you can attain a faith always worthy to be honored by your Lord.

To mimic the centurion's faith, Lord, just speak the words.

Interviewer: This really helps my faith a lot. This is a great subject. I could stay on this subject forever. Why are you laughing?

Wisdom: This part is funny. One final point, "For an angel went down (he came from heaven) at a certain season into the pool of Bethesda, and troubled the water." John 5:4. Think! My son, this is an order from heaven, because no angel would dare function on his own accord. These actions triggered faith in everyone who made it into the pool.

Jesus came alone and felt sorry for a guy who had been there 38 years, who gave up when someone moved ahead of him. Imagine not having executable faith for 38 years? Christ was there to honor the obedience of the angel who had faithfully performed the task he had been assigned. John acknowledges that an angel came from heaven, to work in the earthly environment, and moved attention to the troubled waters; the man should have dived, 38 years before this day, head first into the pool. If he was going to be healed, and if he had broken his neck from the dive, he would have been healed of that as well. If the man stopped when someone moved ahead of him, he didn't want to get wet. To act on faith supersedes reason; reasoning is not an action of faith. Beyond reason is where your faith must begin and no one can get there without meditating and studying the words of Christ... This is why my instructions are better than gold, even fine gold.

Faith is the results generated from knowing, without physical proof, that any miracles, or God inspired messages, were initiated and were first sent from heaven by God. He is rewarding you because of your diligence, persistent, and scope of his righteousness. And "Abraham believed God (had faith), and it was counted unto him for righteousness." Romans 4:3.

Interviewer: I am also cracking up at that story. I remember Jesus said, "This is the work of God, that we believe in Him, whom he has sent." My faith can start there correct?

What is Faith?

Wisdom: Yes, a Mediator exists, you should seek to find him daily.

INTERVIEW SIX
BE FRUITFUL AND MULTIPLY

Interviewer: Why do we have to "be fruitful and multiply"?

Wisdom: My son, it's God's commandment to His entire creation since the beginning, and commandments are meant to be obeyed. To ensure we deliver, the Lord gave you all that pertains to life and godliness.

God is a multiplier; you see what He made out of nothing, a void wasteland. So why wouldn't you create something from nothing? You, who is created in His image and likeness, can do the same. If you're not multiplying His gift within, especially, using my wisdom that is freely approachable to obtain, you're not following His Spirit's command. Remember, He wants multiplication, not addition, subtraction, or division. You can find these commands throughout the scriptures, beginning in

Be Fruitful and Multiply

Genesis. Think about this, there is no purpose to equip male and female with organs to reproduce if the multiplication processing were not expected. I might add one of the Highest rating pleasures you humans enjoy.

In Genesis, the servant of God, Moses, accounted for God's commandment for his creatures, "And God blessed them, putting an ingrained instinct, something they will all know to do, none will have to be taught. Saying, ``Be fruitful, and multiply, and fill the waters in the seas, and let fowl multiply in the earth." Gen 1:22. And the same command to man in verse 28, God blessed them, and God said unto them, be fruitful, and multiply, and replenish the earth, and subdue it. Have dominion over the fish of the sea, and over the fowl of the air, and over every living thing that moves upon the earth." Every living creature was commanded to multiply and reproduce. Meaning that He already knows what you can achieve; God will not tell you to multiply if He didn't give you that ability.

In St John 15, he shares that Christ was planted by the Father, to be planted is to be submerged in the earth. Prior to this submerging was a seed deposited by the Holy Ghost who overshadowed a virgin, one who has never known a man. This seed is inserted in the womb, fertilized and grows to maturity. It is successfully born. Thus, begins to occupy this earth as a child. His journey from heaven now involves a mission to accomplish on behalf of his Father.

One day he decides to enter a temple of the Jews inside he begins to minister from the scrolls containing writings of certain prophets and scribes. Astounded by his knowledge, those who heard him were amazed. Midway, on the journey to his place of residence his parents realized he was missing. They returned to find him only to hear his push back. "Wish ye not that I should be about my Father's business?" Luke 2:49. This indicates Jesus is well aware of the bee-line mission He would accomplish. A destiny with a Cross to die for the sins of all who occupy the Father's creation known as Earth. We now look to Jesus, the author and finisher of our faith, who for the joy that was set before Him, endured the cross, despising the shame, and is set down at the right hand of the throne of God. Hebrews 12:2. While on the cross He ended his destiny with a loud voice "ELI, ELI, LAMA SABACHTHANI"- interpreted as "Why hast thou forsaken me?" Psalm 22:1.

Here is where the husbandman (farmer) has his seed; it will be buried and spring forth out of the earth three days later. Before his resurrection, he takes the power of death, the sting of death from Lucifer to claim all power is His in heaven and earth. As governor of the nations, he establishes a new Law? The Law of the Spirit of Life. YES!! The Father's mission is accomplished. He banishes the old dominant Law, the Law of Sin and Death. Now Jesus as the vine, the Father's vine, a true vine, you and all who will love his appearance are the branches in Him. Christ, even He is required to be fruitful. "Every branch in me that does not bear fruit is cast away and men gather to be burned, but others are pruned to produce more fruits." St John 15:2.

Interviewer: What a story. I understand this much more clearly. Thanks Wisdom.

Wisdom: To date, 2.4 billion people believe in him. Yet it's not enough. Your song, "There's Room At The Cross" says millions have come, yet there is still room for one. You can see multiplication is a spiritual requirement and Jesus has definitely multiplied the amount of The Father's Spirit.

It's not all about childbearing and fruitful harvesting. Remember when Jesus said to his disciples, "look out on the fields to the harvest that are ripe already," Christ refers to the Samaritans coming at the behest of the woman at the well. St John 4:35

When souls for the Lord come His way, He is pleased. This display restored his energy and vitality replenishing no need for nourishment from food.

Interviewer: It would have the same effect on my life. There is plenty of time to dine. Here was a fruitful scene that thrilled the Lord.

INTERVIEW SEVEN
THE HOLY GHOST

This is not intended to be a true likeness of the Holy Spirit.

Interviewer: Who is the Holy Ghost?

Wisdom: The short answer is that He is my boss, in your understanding of authority. But first, answer this question. Does the name, or phrase, Holy Ghost scare you?

Interviewer: No. I'm not mystified by the term.

Wisdom: Son, I reference Genesis 2:7, "And the Lord formed man of the dust of the ground and breathed into his nostrils the breath of life, man became a living soul." Son, every living object, animal, pest, or creature that you enjoy, was recommended to the Father by ministers, and His flames of fire through their gifts helped to create creatures. We had no power to breathe life-giving matter into these creatures, to make any form of life in any one of them. We had to bring our subjects to the Lord God for *Life*. Not even the Holy Ghost, unless designated by the Father, has that power, only the Father and Lord God Jesus possessed that authority.

Interviewer: Gosh, I imagine the world would be much worse if we all had that power. We would be like cartoon characters, evil would be more rampant and disgusting to a God of Love.

Wisdom: Imagine if Lucifer, the disgraced creature, had such authority that he could add to his entourage of evil without limitation. But I say thanks to the Father for reserving this power for Himself. After Christ's ascension into Heaven, Jesus presented Himself to his Father before anyone could touch him. He came back and declared All Power in heaven and earth was given to Him (Matt 28:19). After His resurrection he obtained the power to quicken and raise any being from the dead.

Now I want to show the scriptures where the Spirit of the Lord appeared in a limited role in the anointing and protection scenes. Now familiarize yourself with I Samuel 16, "When the Lord attempts to find a king to govern his people. The Lord rejected all who were brought forward. Until Samuel said to Jesse 'Are these all your sons?' Jesse said he had one more and he was attending the sheep in the fields." David is described in appearance as fair to look upon. The Lord said to Samuel "He is the one, rise anoint him." So the **Spirit of the Lord came upon David** from that time forward. *The Spirit of the Lord came upon David* (1 Samuel 16:13). All of the acts of the Holy Ghost are about being **filled** with the Holy Ghost: it's not about the **Spirit** "to be upon", it's about "being filled within you." Don't miss this point son, it ties into the previous interview. Whatever makes up the Vine flows through to the branches. If a Holy Thing(Lk 1:35) was inside the virgin's womb, authority must be given to all to flow through an indwell (all believers) creating the **like-kind**. A Born Again creature will be to be born of that spiritual seed dwelling inside flesh ,but not of flesh. But of that (Jesus)seed. Today, one should not say "the Spirit of the Lord is upon me," but should say "the Holy Ghost is in me." They will be judged by their fruits.

Interviewer: Please continue {Interviewer sitting on the edge of his seat)

Wisdom: Ask yourself, son, why can't most in church member fellowships today, say to one another.. "have you received the Holy Ghost since you believed? (Acts 19:2-4).

Warning: Pastors, you are robbing the innocent when you don't get an answer from your members regarding the same questions asked in Acts 19:2-4

Is the Holy Ghost not relevant anymore in this generation?

Wisdom continues: son this is why I asked you, does the word Holy Ghost scare you?

All who possess the Holy Ghost must be thankful to possess

Him. They can be judged by their fruit. Because not everyone that says, Lord, Lord will enter the kingdom of God (Matthew 7:21).

Interviewer: Many pastors may be asking the members in private settings, not publicly.

Wisdom: My son, let's hope so. To be in the vine getting pruned and not cut off is better.

This does not mean you have less protection with the Spirit in you...

At the time, the Spirit's presence meant the Lord's protection [upon] David was guarded with the Angels of the Lord, encamped about those that feared him to deliver. The same exists also for believers today. Throughout David's life, protection was needed from most everyone, even his son at one point, and certainly, from Saul, the rejected king of Israel.

But son clearly, the assignment after Christ's ascension for another holy character

The Comforter was to dwell [within] you, which according to Christ is the Holy Ghost.

This is referencing John the Baptist defining how Christ would Baptize.

The difference Jesus emphasized, get this son, the Holy Ghost will not speak of Himself.

Examples:

1) Jesus says "I came down from heaven", the Holy Ghost is silent.

2) Jesus says "all that the Father giveth to me come to me" The Holy Ghost is silent.

3) Jesus says "for I came down from heaven not to do my own will but the Father's will that sent me" the Holy Ghost is silent.

4) Jesus says "And this is the will of Him that sent me, that every one which sees the Son and believes in me shall never see death. (St John 8:51} The Holy Ghost is silent.

5) He that believeth may have everlasting life: and I will raise him up at the last day" St John 6:40, the Holy Ghost is silent.

I could go on with many more examples. And the Holy Ghost will be silent. Because He is not the Only Begotten Son of God.

Interviewer: So, whether upon us or in us God's presence exists?

Wisdom: You did miss the point... If one just says His presence, and not that they are "filled with all joy and peace in believing, so that by the power of the Holy Ghost you may abound in hope". Romans 15:13. The Holy Ghost now exists in this expanded assignment as a Comforter. And charged to do many other things. Son, everything is in the Father's presence. But, If one does not get this [Indwelling presence] They cannot participate in the fruit-bearing process: making them branches that withers and cast into the fire only fit to be gathered and burned.(St John 15:6. It also prolongs your spiritual childhood status to be tossed to and fro and carried about with every wind

The Holy Ghost

of doctrine, by the sleight of men, and cunning craftiness, believers are going to get deceived. Eph 4:14.

Jesus said, "Unless I go away the Father I will not send the Comforter (the Holy Ghost), but if I go he will come." John 16:7. Jesus is making a specific point by using the word "Comforter." He will not say a new Christ will come. Because He foretells that many are coming to say I am Christ, and will deceive many(Matt 24:5)

Yes, one can be comforted by outside relationships. But Jesus knows if you get rejected by others, even by a mother, father, sister, or brother because you believe in Him, the Comfort has to come from within you. Upfront, the Holy Ghost is sealing and insulating you from Carnality from all sides. Eph.1:13.

As I have said, The Father's Kingdom is more organized and much more prolific than any Earthly institution. How much more detail can one be than to number the hairs on a single human's head? I won't get into how sperm is inventoried for conception. It's not that life begins at conception, it's that Eternal Life begins at conception. "No eyes have seen nor ears heard the thing The Father has in store for those who love Him" 1 Corinthians 2:9; these words could describe other things too awesome for mere men to comprehend.

Interviewer: I keep forgetting that the kingdom of God is an institution of great powers.

Wisdom: 99.9% of humanity shares your amnesia and forgetfulness as it relates to the Kingdom of God. Son, I'd like to point to a scene with Gabriel, a mighty representation of God's presence. Beginning with Lk 1:15, He was sent to speak and show Zacharias phenomenal things that would come to pass. Like announcing that John the Baptist who had not been born, is the first son of his body would be filled with the [Holy Ghost] before He comes from His mother's womb. The Holy Ghost would give him a heightened awareness for a Child, making him a gifted protégé of spiritual cognizance and give him recognition as one who would obey the Father's instructions. John the Baptist acknowledged" And I knew him not: but he that sent me to baptize with water, the same said unto me, upon whom thou shall see the Spirit descending, and remaining on him, the same is he which baptized with the Holy Ghost. St John 1:33. Water baptisms are an outer expression of a new Inner work that will follow after Jesus' resurrection. I, Wisdom, was one of John the Baptist's gifts. You gotta see these different phrases or names entering into the Spiritual realm. Gabriel strikes Zacharias with dumbness until after all his predictions had been fulfilled, due to his unbelief. Gabriel didn't tell Zacharias who he was until unbelief reared up. And aren't we very annoyed when priesthood leadership denies heavenly authority? I will mock you.

Interviewer: One good thing about writing down this interview is that I will get to meditate on your wise sayings and by this I especially understand when you only wanted to announce glad tidings.

Wisdom: An additional description of the role of the Holy Ghost happened six months later when God dispatched Gabriel with a new assignment and announcement:

"And in the sixth month the angel Gabriel was sent from God unto a city of Galilee, named Nazareth. To a virgin espoused to a man whose name was Joseph, of the house of David; and the virgin's name was Mary. And the angel came in unto her, and said, 'Hail, thou that

art highly favored, the Lord is with thee: blessed art thou among women.' And when she saw him, she was troubled by what he said, and cast in her mind what manner of salutation this should be. And the angel said unto her, 'Fear not, Mary: for thou hast found favor with God. And, behold, thou shalt conceive in thy womb, and bring forth a son, and shalt call his name Jesus. He shall be great, and shall be called the Son of the Highest: and the Lord God shall give unto him the throne of your father David: and he shall reign over the house of Jacob forever; and of his kingdom there shall be no end.' Then said Mary unto the angel, 'How shall this be, seeing I know not a man?' And the angel answered and said unto her, 'The [Holy Ghost] shall come upon thee, and the power of the Highest shall overshadow thee: therefore also that 'Holy Thing' which shall be born of thee shall be called the Son of God. And, behold, thy cousin Elisabeth, she hath also conceived a son in her old age: and this is the sixth month with her, who was called barren. For with God nothing shall be impossible." Luke 1:26-37

Interviewer: So I see here Mary's personal salutation, "My soul magnifies the Lord, my spirit has rejoiced in God my savior." Luke 1:46. She is honored to be Chosen. Later she exclaims to him that the Gentiles will be blessed and trust in Jesus. Her acceptance is confirmed by this acknowledgment that all generations will call me Blessed (Luke 1:47-48).

Wisdom: Yes! Now my son, I turn your attention to Isaiah's proclamation of Christ.

Elder Johnnie D. Bond, Sr.

"The Spirit of the Lord God is upon me; because the Lord has anointed me to preach good tidings unto the meek; he has sent me to bind up the brokenhearted, to proclaim liberty to the captive and the opening of the prison to them that are bound. To proclaim the acceptable year of the Lord..... At Jesus' opening day starting his fulfillment he stood up in the temple and proclaimed this salutation word for word." Isaiah 61:1

Christ's authority, from the Father's orders, is confirmed by many prophets. Isaiah is one that wrote of Him. Isaiah was in the presence of God when he penned these sacred Words. Elizabeth, when she heard the salutation from Mary, the babe leaped in her womb and she was "filled with the Holy Ghost" Luke 1:41. Now son, turn your attention to Matthew 3:13-17:

"Then cometh Jesus from Galilee to Jordan unto John, to be baptized of him. But John forbade him, saying, I need to be baptized of thee, and comest thou to me? (note John is submitting, humbled by his Lord's presence) And Jesus answering said unto him, 'Suffer it to be so now: for thus it becometh us to fulfill all righteousness.' Then he suffered. And Jesus, when he was baptized, went up straightway out of the water: and, lo, the heavens were opened unto him, and he saw the Spirit of God descending like a dove, and lighting upon him: And lo a voice from heaven, saying, 'This is my beloved Son, in whom I am well pleased.'"

Our emphasis is on what John saw and heard after Christ's ascension from the waters. The Spirit of God descended like a dove setting an approval with physical characteristics and the verbal acknowledgment and designation that Jesus Christ was a Beloved Son (Note: Nothing is required to show the indwelling of the Spirit in Christ. Because Jesus was the epitome of the Father) Without measure was the spirit given to Him,(St John

The Holy Ghost

3:34) This was unheard of in the Spiritual Realm to be preferred above others in the Father's vast kingdom.

You must read, "I will anoint thee with the oil of gladness Above thy fellows". Psalms 45:7. John the Baptist may have wanted assurances later after his imprisonment, but he had no doubts that the one coming after him, now in his presence, whose shoes he was not worthy to unlatch, was the Son of God (John 1:27). The Holy Ghost within John the Baptist helped him to bear witness to the Son of God. It always bears witness; it cannot deny itself.

Interviewer: One would think that John the Baptist and Jesus would have been reared in the same neighborhood and shared nicknames and parties together.

Wisdom: Son, I hope you and others can appreciate how simple our titles and names are. Holy means eternal and it cannot be Holy if its existence is temporary; it must be permanently flawless. Holy as the Father's title means He is Eternal and never-ending. The scriptures acknowledge that Jesus has a name above every name and this denotes his Holy stature (Phil 2:9). Anything that suffers death but returns in its original form is a ghost. So, the name Holy Ghost represents what Jesus Christ accomplished (death, burial, and resurrection), defining the character Holy Ghost, a direct permanent being who will accomplish eight (8) tasks requested by God. Therefore, The Father and Son's decision to provide counsel, comfort, and contentment to all that believe in Him, was to name the Holy Ghost a Comforter and a multi-tasking coordinator.

Interviewer: Wisdom it appears to me, we as believers today, have fallen in the identical trenches of the Scribes and the

Pharisees from Christ's days with Him. We are losing our excitement about the meticulous details so freely provided by the Father and the Son.

This should keep us grateful with comfort supplied or discomfort eased. I am glad for these interviews, they must continue.

Wisdom: My son I have two final points to help understand the difference in a compromise as in Jesus reminded the Pharisees why Moses allowed them to use a writing of divorce. It deviated from God's original commands to leave mother and father and cleave to thy wife. He made them one from the beginning (Mark 10:4-5).

Son, there is no such title as "Trinity" Three equal personalities of the God-Head.

Interviewer: Whoa, Explain?

Wisdom: My son here is where the spiritual wrecking ball swings obliterating Ignorance.

The answer to three (3) words. first Only, second Begotten, third Son.

1) Only: as an adverb: No one or nothing more besides, solely or exclusively.

> now as an adjective: Alone of its kind, single or solitary.

2) Begotten: Of, or from a parent, the father's seed, making it equal to or with him.

3) Son: let's use Gabriel's angel definition to Mary: "That [holy thing] which shall be born of thee shall be called the Son of God"

The Holy Ghost

All definitions have to be true and applied to everyone to be what "Trinity" Implies, Having Obtained Equality. The Jews noted "He said God was His Father making himself [equal] with God; because salvation is of the Jews. They wanted to stone Jesus for that statement. (St John 5:18)

Wisdom Speaks: Show me in scriptures Jesus the [Only] Son and right beside that statement, show me Holy Ghost the [Only] son.{St John 1:18a}

Next Show me...the only [Begotten] Son, which is in the bosom of the Father...{St John 1:18b}.

right beside that statement show me Holy Ghost is the only [Begotten] son which is in the bosom of the Father.

Lastly, show me "No man hath seen God at any time; the only begotten Son, which is in the bosom of the Father has declared him St John 1:18. Show me where the Holy Ghost is asked to make such a claim? We (I Wisdom, Knowledge, Prudence etc..) are all in the presence of God daily, as his ministers, his flames of fire we would never, I mean Never take a position that was not given to us. the Holy Ghost included. If the Voice had never declared Jesus as the ONLY BEGOTTEN

JESUS WOULD STILL BE CONTENT WITH THE GLORY HE HAD WITH THE FATHER FROM THE BEGINNING With NO such title that denotes He is an Only Begotten of the Father. The Voice from heaven in the mountain confirmed this posture for Jesus among three (3) witnesses, Peter James and John. Enough witnesses to confirm as Moses Law required. The compromise of (Matthew 19:8)Moses with divorce papers allowed by

God, because of the hardness of man's heart he allowed; just as your leader decries the Holy Ghost has equality?.

Son, the Holy is content with His title Comforter.

a) He will tell you he never died for anyone sins

b) He will tell you he has never suffered in His celestial body form.

c) He has never been ashamed.

d) He will tell you he has never hung on a cross.

e) He will tell you he has never eaten a piece of broil fish.

the list goes on. Seriously, son we in heaven do not take positions when not given or assigned to us. That is what is meant by the Lord possessed me at the beginning of His way Proverb 8:22. That he called me; If He doesn't call you, do not come to Him.

What your leadership is doing they are trying to put forth important authority that is given out only by the Father, trying in a futile attempt to allow a usurping spirit to seep into the Father's Superiority, Preeminence, and Sovereignty. They need to say what Christ said about the coming again of Himself at the end of his work, to emphasize God's dominance; Jesus from His lips said "But of that day and hour knoweth no man, no, not the angels of heaven, but my Father only".... Matthew 24:36)

Try to get the Holy Ghost or even myself to tell you the day and hour that the Lord will execute judgment on sinners and we will Laugh at you. I mean out loud Laughing. I "Wisdom is justified of all my children" (Luke 7:35). A great compliment from our Lord. Thank you, Lord! I Wisdom did not raise a fool.

Now understand the manifestation and fulfillment of a promised event.

Acts 2:1-4 should not be treated as the only prerequisite doctrine to obtain access to the Indwelling of the Holy Ghost; it was simply a manifestation and fulfillment of a promise that the Holy Ghost would be sent by Christ Himself.

The Holy Ghost

Jesus so defines in St John 14:16 and 26; St John 15:26, John 16 He states clearly.

The role of the Holy Ghost:

1. He is the Spirit of Truth.

2. He will guide in all truth.

3. He shall not speak of Himself.

4. He speaks about the things he hears.

5. He shows you things to come.

6. He reproves the world of sin, of righteousness, and judgment.

7. He brings all things to remembrance

8. He glorifies Jesus. I really want to emphasize this one. Glorify himself? No. He glorifies Jesus, Jesus!

These points and others detail the role of the Holy Ghost that no single act, in The Acts of the Apostles was to add a foreign language to your vocabulary.

To just speak in tongues. He has a much greater role within all Believers when they accept the Lord Jesus.

This dovetails into everything we have discussed to emphasize the Humility from the hosts of heaven to the Savior who constantly declared "I came down from heaven not to do my own will but the will of my Father that sent me". When men attempt to show their so-called holy ghost power. Ask yourself. Why would the Holy Ghost as he clearly understands only the humble will be exalted; Why would men exalt or glorify themselves?

Or, why would the Holy Ghost promote or exalt a mere man at all if he understands

men's role as ministers is the same as Christ's, to serve. Getting the most done behind the scenes. Jesus warned against functioning out of the gentile's hierarchy standards.

. He said the greatest among you is your servants Matt 23:11?

Remember Lucifer has a great congregation declared he would exalt his throne above the stars of God Isa.14:13.

But I know he will be thrust down into the pit I helped dig.

There is no way one can pray to Mary and be in conformity with God's purpose. There is no way one can pray to the Holy Ghost and be in conformity with God's purpose. He shall glorify me: for he shall receive of mine, and shall show it unto You. St John 16:14.

In these eight (8) instances, Jesus describes the role of the Holy Ghost.

The Holy Ghost, one who we in the Father's orbit and existence appreciate

He's not seeking glory or personal adulation or obsequious flattery.

As He was designated in this important role to complete your redemption process.

To obtain the Holy Ghost just begin to meditate on the word of God.

The words of Jesus will start up the relationship, nothing wild or mystical.

He Comforts you out of the word/Gospel message from Christ. Again, this comfort takes place within you, that's why you have to get something in you from the pages or the Voice of an Alexander Scourby reading, and my preference is the King James Version.

The Holy Ghost

The Lord is near the brokenhearted and saves such to be of a contrite spirit. He Comforts you out of the words of Jesus' gospel message. This my son is why Christ said blasphemy of this personality is unpardonable. One may offend Christ through one's ignorance but rejection of your final consulate (the Holy Ghost) to heaven is unacceptable.

Wisdom concludes this interview: *Again, my appreciation as I Wisdom Speaks is a gift of the Holy Ghost, Himself.*

My son Jesus' appearance at his coming will prove this quote:

He is the "Son who sent the Holy Ghost and the One who pleased the Father".

<u>**Interviewer:**</u> *Wisdom please! I will not interrupt you. Explain how I or one can Receive the HOLY GHOST?*

HOLY GHOST RECEIVED

Begin this search knowing; As I Wisdom Speaks, I am without hypocrisy, to be half-hearted in this effort nullifies my instructions to you.

Also, the Holy Ghost is the Spirit of Truth he can't or will never lie to you. You're safe to receive this knowledge.

We will first share a few scriptures that will affirm and show that The Father and Son wants all believers to have this promise. The Holy Ghost!

Please often review the Interviewer's subject with me. Who is the greatest in the kingdom;.

That interview is a must to read, study, and embrace to remain in harmony with your goal to walk in the spirit...

The Who is the greatest Interview Is visibly the understanding how

Elder Johnnie D. Bond, Sr.

although great. All Angels that exist in heaven today are always in subjection to the Father. So, all believers beginning as babes must remain humble, to progress to the fullness of a Christ maturity. Become a Meek candidate and inherit the earth as your reward. No one else can change or hinder your success, to reach this goal, only becoming an unbeliever can nullify what I have instructed you to do. Getting a little knowledge without all the truth is just as dangerous as never having received this knowledge.

And you will be a fool that hates Knowledge if you refuse it.

Observe the acronyms of S.A.V.E.D EXPLAINED: (S) See-(A) Acknowledge-(V) Value-(E) Enter (D) Delivered.

The (S)?.

Except a man be Born Again, he cannot {SEE} the kingdom the kingdom of God. St John 3:3.

Just to See the kingdom, Jesus said, requires a Spiritual Conversion.

God is a Spirit: and those that worship Him must worship him in Spirit and Truth's (St John 4:24) All experiences are what Jesus described as the blowing wind. No laying on of men's hands or spitting at the mouth.**This birth is of God; as God controls when it cometh. Be sincere, pray and wait. Knowing that patience possesses your soul.

Both scriptures emphasize that spiritual insight and control must exist to communicate with The Father This is only accomplished by a personal experience and the believers are rewarded when they commit themselves to this advice from Christ's own words.

. "But thou, when thou pray (impetrating), enter any Room alone, in a vehicle, or any enclosed area alone.

(My suggestion take a personal small child photo in the room to pray

75

The Holy Ghost

for that little one in the

photo) Yes, you are praying for yourself. then shut your door then pray to your Father (for the Father seeketh such to worship Him (St John 4:23).

He is also in your secret place with you, "and your Father who Sees in Secret will reward you openly" Matt 6:6. And He (Jesus) breathed on them and spoke. Receive you the Holy Ghost. St John 20:22.

I Wisdom taught my interviewer to take Alexander Scourby's voice in scriptures into his closet, his vehicle, as one of his secret closets, to meditate on the word, to pray, rejoice in songs of praise to the Father.

And please readers take note of this example. You will see what has happened for him.

The Father is rewarding him openly to Bless His People with all interviews that will be shared with you and your loved ones. Now. First, look at the emphasis on the letter {S} to See?

(Paraphrased) See-We must believe the testimony of John the Baptist.

He said I didn't personal know Jesus, "but, he that sent me, said whom thou shall [See] the Spirit descending on, the same is He which will Overshadow, Overwhelm, Baptize with the Holy Ghost (St John 1:33-34)

Note: This Baptism is Something Christ does for the believer to become a son or daughter.

Which are born, not of blood, nor of the will of the flesh, nor of the will of man, but of God (St John 1:13) "But of God" (**Look back into the upper quotes where I told you that already**)

Again, John the Baptist say: And I [Saw] and bare record that this is the Son of God]

God has given all of us spiritual eyes. In your mind's eye, take a moment to go there, go there with John the Baptist to look at Jesus' a "Only Begotten sent from heaven to become a Son of Man to go to His death on a cross.

So that the One who sent Him (The Father) could reconcile the world back to Himself.

Recap:

a) John the Baptist's testimony. I saw and bare record

b) Jesus said the witness of two men are True (St John 8:17)

c) Along with John, The Father And the Son both bare record that Jesus is the Son of

God.(St John 8:18)

Second, (A) to Acknowledge?.

Having one's sight on something doesn't mean that they Acknowledge what they have observed. So, Acknowledgement is important.

(Paraphrased) (1) Acknowledge- Nathaniel answered and said unto Him,

"Rabbi, you are the Son of God; you are the king of Israel. (St John 1:49)

(2) Acknowledge--And Simon Peter answered and said, Thou art the Christ. the Son of the living God.

Believe Nathaniel and Peter's affirmation: Jesus is the Christ, the Son of the living God

(Matthew 16:16)

Third--(V) to Value for You?

to See and Acknowledge one must now determine the Value?

(Paraphrased) Here,'the kingdom of heaven is like a merchant man, seeking goodly pearls, when he had found one pearl of great price, went and sold all that he had, and bought it" (Matt 13:45-46) *Again, the worth and Value you place on getting into Christ's dwelling place and even His presence daily; where a mansion awaits each of His believers'* (John 14:2)

Weigh the Value then, pledge, obligate, dedicate some time daily, even hourly, to a secret closet experience.

This is earnest money toward your Value and Worth.

Fourth, (E) to Enter Into...

Not everyone that saith to me Lord, lord shall Enter the kingdom of heaven...?

(Matt 7:21a)

Get full assurance you aren't one of those. Do the will of His Father in Heaven. (Matt 7:21b)

(Paraphrased) To Enter: "Jesus answered, except a man be born of Water and of the Spirit

he cannot Enter into the kingdom of God. Except a man who is to be [given spiritual life]

Born of—Water,ie.."But whosoever drinketh of the Water that I shall give him shall never thirst; but the Water that I shall give him shall be in him a well of Water springing up into everlasting life. (St John 4:14) *note: (This is not a dirty pond or clean pool water, you're not a fish)*

This Water is not a colorless, transparent, odorless liquid. It's a Water

Elder Johnnie D. Bond, Sr.

given by Christ Himself. (St John 3:5 -John 4:14)

Again, He that believeth on me, as the scripture hath said, out of his belly shall flow rivers of Living Water (St John 7:38). Note the belly is a storage tank, like a memory bank, He (Holy Ghost will teach you all things and bring all things to your remembrance, whatsoever I have said unto you" (St John 14:26). Bringing what's stored in the belly, memory, (like food in the belly providing nutrition upon demand) will feed the soul.

Creating the hunger and thirst effect, In Jesus's own words.(St John 7:38) also highlights here more emphasis on the word Flow. River waters always flow downward indicating it is alive and purest as it flows. Also coming from heaven is always a downward action and activity for believers.

Your prayer in the secret closet goes up ward triggering a downward flowing to start personal communication, resulting in blessings out of the Spirit and Life words of Christ constantly flowing from heaven's FLOOD GATE! (St John 6:63)

When one reaches this state of consciousness they have Entered. One has now Entered and is now seated while still on earth in heavenly places in Christ Jesus.(Eph. 2:6)

Fifth,(D) Delivered from evil:

Here overcoming power is needed to defeat the Accuser of your soul.

The Holy Ghost as Comforter is in you, He is the greater in you than he that is in the world

(1 John 4:4). Therefore, one is Delivered. Resist the Devil and he will flee. Put on the whole armor of God. Eph.6:11-18.

(Paraphrased) (D) Delivered from death, hell, and the grave.

"I will ransom them from the power of the grave; I will redeem them *from death;...(Hosea 13:14)*

O death, where is thy sting? O grave where thy victory is. 1 Corinthians 15:45

Any believers who trust after hearing these words of truth, the gospel of your salvation, in whom also after you believed, you are sealed with the Holy Ghost of promise.Eph.1;13

Again, do not grieve the Holy Ghost of God, by whom you were sealed unto the of day of redemption.(Eph. 4:30

Rehash often:

A)   *See Him*

B)   *Acknowledge Him often*

C)   *Value His love and mercy,especially forgiveness of any sin committed daily.*

D)   *Enter into His gates with praise to bless His name!*

E)   *Delivered Take heed unto thyself,and unto the doctrine; continue in them: for in doing this you shall both save thyself, and those that hear thee. You are fruitful and S.A.V.E.D*

After observing my instructions here and as they are adhered to.

One will be able to say with a loud boisterous voice of affirmation when asked "have you received the Holy Ghost since you believed? The thunderous answer is Yes!Yes!................ I Wisdom Speaks

Wisdom concludes this interview.

BRIEF CHAT ONE
THE JUDGES

Interviewer: Who are the Judges?

Wisdom: My son, they are numerous and Jesus mentioned their duties. Remember Peter's question? "What shall we have, seeing that we have left all to follow you?" Matthew 19:27. I mean, the personal level the disciples felt around the savior, the Lord of lords we're talking about here, is astounding. No angelic being would ever have such a personal selfish thought, let alone a question.

Peter wants to know the guarantee that after leaving everything (his fishing career) behind, how will he become successful? To bring this disciple to his senses Christ three (3) times questioned Peter's Love for His eternal purpose of redemption. Christ says in a low, tranquil tone, "Peter loveth thou me more than these???" while referring to fishes (John 21:15). Was Peter asking for assurance, or an opportunity to cut bait and move on? I'll tell ya, he was expecting earthly rewards.

Interviewer: Peter, an older brother of Andrew, who brought him to Jesus, may have believed he would jeopardize the family (fishermen) business if he gave too much of his time to a ministry of a Galilean carpenter.

Wisdom: Yes, Mrs. Zebedee also tried to lobby Jesus with worship and flattery; she requested coveted positions for her sons, Andrew and John, she wanted them to sit on the right and left hand of His power. Matt 20:21

My son, note what you will witness here: Jesus always acknowledged the superiority of the Father. In your vernacular and respect for the boy's mom, He says, "ma'am, the position is not mine to give but my Father's" (Mark 10:40). She had risked further dissent among an already doubtful group; as awkward as they were, most of the disciples surrounding Christ remained on the journey with Him. In the end, Christ acknowledged, without reservation, that they, His disciples, had been hand-picked by the Father and that He had only lost one, the son of perdition (St. John 17:12).

Interviewer: What prompted this engagement?

Wisdom: They witnessed Christ's demands from a wealthy man. The rich young ruler could not meet a full commitment and the young rich ruler went away sorrowful. Matt 19:22. So, they begin jogging, for temporary earthly stature; they were sure Christ would eventually attain a kingdom on earth and restore all things unto the House of David.

The disciples heard many words and were assured they would soon be in some type of governing authority because they thought the people would soon swoop in to make Him a king. Check out these comments about Christ, the people, and leaders alike:

- *"No man can do these things except God be with Him."*
- *"Thinkest not that I should not be about my Father's business."*
- *"They sought to kill Him but they feared the people for all recognized him as a Prophet." "Thinkest thou that I cannot now pray to my Father and he will give me 12 legions of angels."*
- *"Moses gave you not that bread from heaven, but my Father giveth you the true Bread from Heaven. For the bread of God is He that cometh down from heaven, and giveth life unto the world."*
- For they were about five thousand (5,000) men. *"And he said to his disciples, " Make them sit down by fifties in a company."*

Peter began wondering what was left of the most important positions available? And, who was next in line? As always, Christ's thoughts are so above those of human thoughts. He began to share the ultimate eternal role for the students who would Drink of the cup and be Baptized with His identical baptism—signifying what death they shall die. Peter wanted to secure his value one way or the other; if it was now, you would say he was trying to weigh the risk and ROI.

Interviewer: Will angels judge men?

The Judges

Wisdom: No, Jesus is the son of man, and just as peers judge you in your society, Christ is your equal and will judge you. The Father has committed all judgment to the Son because he is the Son of man. St John 5:22. Jesus often scolded Pharisees, "Do not think that I will accuse you of the Father: there is one that accuses you, even Moses, in whom you trust." St John 5:45.

Jesus then takes all the disciples, even Peter, from the earthly position of power, saying to them, "Verily I say unto you, that ye which have followed me. In the regeneration when the Son of man shall sit on the throne of his glory. Ye shall sit upon twelve thrones, judging the twelve tribes of Israel." Matt 19:28.

Interviewer: What a tremendous role Jesus gives lowly disciples, making them judges as peers and especially of their own heritage.

Wisdom: Son, these are the last days. The perilous times are here. The great cloud of witnesses that exist and those that will endure to the end, to receive crowns having borne hardness as a good soldier of Christ. As disciples now, you too are the ones that are going to be Judges and Witnesses. The Holy Ghost judges the world daily, and is of judgment, because the prince of this world is Judge. He judges all those that offend you daily. John 16:11. You will be witnesses as the Bride (Church) for her groom, even Christ.

Interviewer: Acting as a judge or witness will serve the same purpose. In our court of Laws both factors to establish a final Judgment.

Elder Johnnie D. Bond, Sr.

Wisdom: My son. Let me speak now more to those chosen by the Father for a unique and important task in His redemption plans. May be seen as an under the radar type of action.

But I have stated the meticulous activity and how God leaves no stone unturned. Watch what successes God has already accomplished that takes a spiritual discernment to understand.

Remember Proverb 21:1 "The King's heart is in the hand of the Father, as the rivers of water he turned it whithersoever He will? King James, A King of royalty in one of the early nations established in the years of the Lord 1604-11, translated the Holy Bible from Greek and Hebrew Scrolls to English. It stands, even now, as the best-selling document of all times. Therefore, this Holy Book, your Bible, will stand against anyone who claimed that the word of God wasn't accessible, or they didn't understand the language. King James authorized 41 scribes after the Father turned and instructed his heart to translate His sacred Word from Hebrew and Greek to English. King James, no doubt will be called forward to help judge and witness against those that say the Father's Gospel was not available in their languages. Just the King's presence will condemn those that make such a claim. Therefore, anyone who pleads ignorance of King James's Bible he will be there to dispute their claims.

Interviewer: A King with a profound assignment. I see the Father has already done things, completed tasks that undercut millions who will come with Excuses.

Wisdom: Another one of the Father's servants with a similar mission is Alexander Scourby; his gifted voice reads word for word the printed, sacred, and Holy Bible words. He will witness against those who say, "I could not read or understand His

The Judges

Gospel message preached in all the world before the end." Alexander's voice will stand as a judgment against them. His voice will be louder and more prolific than ever to dispute their claims. Even when set against leaders who preach a doctrine of men who are not promoting the Voice of Heaven.

Interviewer: What then Wisdom, will allow many to escape these judges and witnesses?

Wisdom: Glad you asked. Fruit-bearing and remaining good fruit, allows believers to escape judgment. You shall be known by your fruit. Therefore, *continue to pray that Your Fruits Remains* make sure you help them to hear the words of Christ, Then He will say to those servants, "Well done thy good and faithful servant you have ruled well over a few things, I will now make you rulers over many. Enter now into the joy of your Lord." Matt. 25:23.

BRIEF CHAT TWO
WOMEN

Interviewer: What about the women; those women who had an intricate role in God's redemptive plan?

Wisdom: Well, my son, there are three women I'd like to briefly discuss today. I always give my Instructions from my spiritual authority. It is written, *"The first Adam was made a living soul; the last Adam was made a Quickening Spirit."* I Corinthian 15:45. (A Quickening Spirit is a life giving spirit and can raise the dead A.K.A. JESUS.) Without Eve, this is not possible. Adam named the first woman "Eve" because she would be the mother of humanity and the metaphorical mother of all living things (Genesis 3:20). The first Adam in 1 Cor 15:45, wasn't negating the presence of the woman, he was celebrating what was to come, the creation of a perfectly executed redemptive plan (the death, burial, and resurrection of Jesus).

Interviewer: Wisdom, this insite helps me understand the perfection of God's plan for salvation. As I well know, procreation happens when a male and a female submit to His command, "Be fruitful and multiply;" with, which is an ingrained instinct, there to form another living soul.

Wisdom: My Son, disobedience of a Godly command by any subject, whether beguiled by omission or commission, that takes a fruit from a tree of knowledge, of good and evil, and consumes it did alter their position in Eden, the paradise garden. Thus, God thrust them out to work and punished Adam by forcing him to generate sweat on his brow, to eat bread and punished Eve by coloring her childbirth with pain (even though she would rejoice when the experience ended). And from a woman-child's womb, Mary, the Last Adam came, the Quickening Spirit Adam (A.K.A. Jesus), who shares a dual sonship status, a binary ranking as Son of Man and Son of God. His sole authority equivalent to that of the Father. Jesus has the authority to speak and revive life to anything or anyone, just as the Father (John 11:43-44). At the garden scene God to protect man from the tree of life, to keep man from living in a cursed nature. He placed fire-flaming swords to prevent Adam and Eve from entering the paradise garden again.

Interviewer: Women make all this happen. We don't get the like kind of seed bearing without them. We don't get the savior who will reconcile the world back to the Father.

What a fantastic role God designed for them!

Wisdom: Correct. They are very essential to the Father' master plan. I was proficient at setting traps for the Father's pleasure. The enemy needed bait and I destroyed him in a trap.

Elder Johnnie D. Bond, Sr.

This trap lead to Christ, called the woman's seed, will crush the head of Lucifer and only come away with a bruised heel (Genesis 3:15).

Interviewer: In his own words John records, "For as the Father raises the dead, and quickeneth them; even so the Son quickeneth whom he will" St John 5:21.

Wisdom: And again he says, "For as the Father hath life in Himself; so hath He given to the Son to have life in himself." St John 5:26. This equivalence is only afforded to the Son, Jesus. I hope you can see the reality of these statements as evidence that He walked on earth. No other force or spiritual authority exists with this type of dominance; this is a life-giving superiority. This is what baffled all occupants in heaven - One fellow out of many with this awesome Authority - yet, we accepted this unanimously.

Never forget the words in these two scriptures.

Let's go further.

Interviewer: Besides Eve, what other women of importance are used in God's puzzle of creation?

Wisdom: So, next, the Father decided to use Mary, a seed of David, a virgin, and a cousin of Elizabeth (who was in her old-age, yet set to conceive as well), as a favored vessel through which the Son would come physically into the Earth.

But. Also a caution, my son, read this exchange;

"While the Pharisees were gathered together, Jesus asked them, "What do you think about the Messiah? Whose son is he?" "The son of David," they replied. He said to them, "How is it then that David, speaking by the Spirit, calls him 'Lord'?"

Matthew 22:41-44. For he says, "The Lord said to my Lord, 'Sit at my right hand until I put your enemies under your feet.'" Psalms 110:1.

Likewise, Mary exclaims in Luke 1:48-50:

"For he hath regarded the low estate of his handmaiden: for, behold, from henceforth all generations shall call me blessed. For he that is mighty hath done to me great things; and holy is his name. And His mercy is on them that fear him from generation to generation."

So, Mary never asked for such praise. When she looked upon Jesus on His cross, "He said to [John] the disciple, 'Behold your mother!' And from that hour that disciple took her to his own home." John 19:27. His coming was never owed to any other being. *He is the resurrection power alone* (John 11:27).

Interviewer: We know the beloved John was a disciple who lays in the bosom of Christ, and if David is called "a man after God's own heart," then John would be the disciple who "heard the heartbeat of God." This responsibility of taking-in Mary, the mother of Jesus, into his home, was a great remembrance of Christ's acknowledgement of her place in the Father's redemptive plan.

Wisdom: Speaking of memorializing a woman, the woman that anointed Jesus' body in preparation for His death is remembered; Jesus said, "Verily I say unto you, wheresoever this gospel shall be preached in the whole world, there shall also this, that this woman hath done, be told for a memorial of her" Matthew 26:13. Jesus personally, memorialized and acknowledged her as the one who prepared Him for his Exit (death), and Mary as the one chosen for His Entrance (birth), showing women, like Eve, that all are important, and essential parts of His creation.

Interviewer: Wisdom, I appreciate how you show that women are essential, now what about His brethren?

Wisdom: Jesus said to his brethren of His mother, "The world cannot hate you; but me it hates, because I testify of it, that the works thereof are evil" St John 7:7. Here you see It will always be easy to fill one's conversation with someone other than Jesus. "For this is the condemnation, that light is come into the world, men love darkness rather than light because their deeds are evil".(St John 3:19)

When Jesus initially appeared on the scene; he grabbed cords and beat the money changers out of the temple as a warning to all. Ungodly zeal can eat you up. Shun the hype, keep your focus on Him as suggested by the Voice from heaven.

Another point I'd like to emphasize is:

"While he still talked to the people, behold, his mother and his brethren stood without, desiring to speak with him. Then one said unto him, Behold, thy mother and thy brethren stand without, desiring to speak with thee. But he answered and said unto him that told him, Who is my mother? and who are my brethren? And he stretched forth his hand toward his disciples, and said, Behold my mother and my brethren! For whosoever shall do the will of my Father which is in heaven, the same is my brother, and sister, and mother." Matt 12:46-50.

He did not do much [healing] work where He lived because of the Jewish People's unbelief. They always focused on His Earthly parents more than His true origin. "I came down from heaven" and showed the level of their disbelief. God's sovereignty and dominance must remain Holy. My Son, God doesn't share His space with anyone. Christ acknowledged this with, "Why callest thou me good? There is only one good, that is the Father." Matt 19:17.

Lucifer attempts to occupy the same place with Him and all will see his end.

Let us continue this conversation in another interview.

Interviewer: Yes! I have many more questions on this subject.

BRIEF CHAT THREE
THE CHILDREN

Interviewer: Wisdom, what about the Children?

Wisdom: The Children? Oh yes, the future. One of the reasons I agreed to this Interview is that I See great potential for the Children with these series. First, we teach them how to number their days, then we teach them how to apply their hearts unto wisdom. Psalm 90:12 Backing up also to "Have a heart that is steadfast to love our God. "Psalm 78:6-8

Interviewer: I'm hopeful that together we'll create a generation that will obey His words of Christ in a copy of every article, book, or lecture from you, Wisdom, you will bless them. You have said "I love them that love me, and those that seek you early shall find Me." Pro.8:17.

The Children

Wisdom: My son, every purpose of the Father begins in His mind. He searches for a suitable couple to carry out His will. Elizabeth and Zacheriah are quick examples, they brought forth John the Baptist.

Also, remember how early a child's relationship begins with Jesus, Saying to Jeremiah. "Before I formed thee in the belly I knew thee, and before thou camest forth out of the womb I sanctified thee, and I ordained thee a prophet unto the nations." Jeremiah 1:5.

I have an important message to drill into your head; please read the scripture below and always lock into your mind the phrase "***Which Believe In Me***":

- "But whoso shall offend one of these little ones "***which believe in me*** ", it were better for him(the offender) that a millstone were hanged about his neck, and that he were drowned in the depth of the sea" Matthew 18:6.

You may recall the evil one wanted to defeat the purpose of the Father at Christ's Birth? It prompted the Father to send His angel to Joseph in a dream, "Arise, take the young child and his mother, and flee into Egypt, and be there until I bring thee word; for Herod seeks the young child to destroy him." Matthew 2:13. My son, you are aware that all souls belong to the Lord; but the soul that sinneth will die. To escape death, *believe in me*, in the Son is Paramount. Therefore, protection and warnings and severe punishment here,as Jesus described in Matthew, is suitable for offenders.

Interviewer: Does that mean that when the child grows up, he will no longer be qualified for this promise?

94

Wisdom Speaks: No. He wasn't just talking about the child's physical stature. He was talking about the Seed of Faith that is in the child; it must be given unimpeded progression to grow to the stature and fullness of Christ. Children are tender and lowly at heart, if fed the word of God and seek after me early, prosperity awaits at their doors. Solomon quotes me verbatim in Proverbs 8:18, "That is what is expected of you. That state of the heart. A tender heart. A heart that depends on the Father for everything is entitled to THE PROSPERITY AND PROTECTION PLAN OF HEAVEN." Yet, abuses will come at the ages of adolescents, teens, adults, or seniors. Would you abuse the child at any stage?.

Interviewer: No. I Love them dearly.

Wisdom: I'm sure you won't. I'm also sure that you will go all out to punish anyone that hurts your child. That's the way the Father is too; anyone that hurts a believer, from the womb to old-age, receives a swift and severe punishment without exception.

Wisdom gives her instructions here:

All who desire to see life changing prosperity for you and your Family: attach a very early childhood picture of You below, add to one of the postcards. Often gaze at this photo and stare intensely at the whole being; look for insight that leads up to their conception. God's purpose will be fulfilled. Offer unbridled praise for Him who brought you forward to this day; He is worthy, who called you into His light. See the miraculous events surrounding you.

The Children

You were born into an Eternal Kingdom. Yes! It is so. Appreciate this miracle more. Marvel that your future was planned for Eternity.

Loving-kindness, and tender-mercy strolled you down Earth's terrain, avoiding obstacles to approach blameless, and covered in Jesus's blood to approach Throne of the King.

Now You are His! Be honored to be Chosen a Friend and not a Servant.

Always honor father and mother upon the earth, but learn to depend on the true Father for provisions and mercy all the days of your existence on this Earth. Expect and await the coming of your Lord.

Interviewer: Wisdom, it's sad to say but my parents never advised me to pray for myself. I believe it would have done wonders for my self esteem in the low points of my life. Thanks Wisdom. God does have a unique purpose beginning as babes for every soul that he breathes into the breath of Life. He wants to make each of us an heir and joint heir with the Only Begotten of the Father. His name is Jesus, the sweetest name in heaven and earth.

We will more than multi-multiply the Host that fell from heaven as lightning. We are each other's fruit. "And they,continuing daily with one accord in all places,and breaking bread from house to house,did eat their meat with gladness and singleness of heart.Praising God,and having favor with all the people. And the Lord added to the church daily such a should be S.A.V.E.D".

Elder Johnnie D. Bond, Sr.

The Children

Practical: Attach a very early childhood picture of you here.

Elder Johnnie D. Bond, Sr.

Practical: Attach a picture of a loved one here.

Elder Johnnie D. Bond, Sr.

Blank space

Use at your discretion.

Elder Johnnie D. Bond, Sr.

Adopt This Affirmation:

I, _____your name_____, *am a child of God, and have overcome the works of the enemy of my soul through Christ and the Holy Ghost's guidance. Because greater is He that is in me, than he that is in the world. God is mindful of me. He takes care of all that concerns me. I am marvelously and wonderfully made. I believe in His Son. I am a child of His glory. My Father is Jealous of me and will punish, with the harshest of punishment, anyone who seeks to obstruct my path to His abundant Life.* I AM A CHILD OF GOD. *The devil is a defeated foe. He may roar but I dwell in the secret place of the Highest and I abide under the shadow of the Almighty.*

Make this affirmation every day until you come into the consciousness of this reality. Teach your offspring and their children to their endless generations.

As a parent:

- Teach your children through your experiences and hide nothing.

- Teach them how you overcame it.

- Teach them how to believe in Jesus Christ.

- Teach them why they are precious to God. Let them know that God has a Protective Love towards them.

- Teach them that they are the apple of His eye any evil one's attempts at destruction will not prosper.

Pray for and with them every day with words of affirmation. While in your presence, ask them to pray for themselves and their parents. Add a childhood photo of you first, then of them (on the next page), in your book and point to it as they pray for themselves. Knowledge of God in the mouth of babes and sucklings is perfect praise.

Teach the young ones that whenever they are overwhelmed by the roaring of the devil, mentally, physically, or otherwise, to call on the Lord Jesus; His name alone summons the angels encamped about them to deliver them from fear. Teach them that peers are not all taught to believe, but to seek every opportunity to win them to the Light. Have them tell a friend that there is one who rejoices over them with songs of deliverance.

Teach them that He is the good shepherd that takes care of all His sheep; even those that could stray. He will never allow any evil force to tear them apart.

Teach them that the Father loves them with an Everlasting Love. Teach them that His Quicken Spirit assures them of eternal life. Make it their goal to win friends for Him, as fruit for the kingdom, as they too can have the Life of Christ.

Do not forget that even as an adult you also need these words, and when you teach these things, you have the mind of Christ.

My son, we will exhaust this subject in our next Interview.

A BLESSED FAMILY

I share this photo of my family because I want my readers to see in real time that **His will for me** was initiated from my ancestors, how-and-when the Father started His Purpose for my life. His purpose was to raise up one who He qualified to be a recipient, a willing vessel, to help open the understanding of sinners who will believe during this redemption timetable.

A Blessed Family

Jesus tells the woman at the well that we know what we worship for, Salvation for the Jewish People. Rather than say Jewish People, I would like to say First born because Shem was the first born of Noah which started the next generation of humanity after the flood.

Shem, offsprings are Jewish People. Unbelievers, you can stop hating on Jewish People, they are just big brothers. Think of a household and its parents, most of the time responsibility falls first to the eldest child,God's order is no different. He will give the first duty and blessing to Abraham a Son of Shem also.Thou,He shall enlarge Japheth (Gentiles) Jesus Will Come via the seed of David. Again, of first born status.

Here is part of my origin according to my DNA; I am 13% percent Jewish, a dominant feature. My great grandfather is a Jewish son who married my great grandmother of African heritage, and they reproduced my grandmother Beatrice Taylor. She married Daniel Hafford and they produced Beatrice Hafford, who is my mother, the beautiful woman standing in the midst of the six children, Mrs. Beatrice Bond, my Mom. She is doing what moms do, educating her brood. Five here are her children.

Jesus says if one of these in this photo who believes in him is offended a millstone necktie would be in their future.

From left to right: Joseph, Michael, Vonzetta, (A.K.A. Michael O., a cousin) and William, the oldest brother, who stands on my mother's left, and I am sitting last in the frame, very engaged with my toy.

The Father's unction at work even then in this photo,… listening for 48 years to Alexander Scourby's old and new testament readings. Help me understand He controls the vessels unto honor and those unto dishonor.

The **W**ill and the **D**o of His pleasure is manifested in my life. I am humbled. This is the Lord's Doing!

We are a Blessed Family.

IN CONCLUSION

I thank you, Father.

Your word says, in Romans 8:28, "We know that all things work together for good to them that love God, to them who are called according to his purpose." Paul's tells the Romans "It's not of him that willeth, nor of him that runneth, but the lord that showeth mercy. "Romans 9:16

Father, to show me no one dies and is perished forever, in 1975 you allowed me to witness my mother's departure from Earth (death), there in a garden as I called out to go with her, she said, "You have to go back." She repeated this statement twice. And now I see why I should stay back, because there's more work to be done.

Secondly, your glowing hand appeared to me in the thick of darkness in my prison cell, with lights out at 10 pm, a place and time no one expected "goodness." And Father, from your Wisdom in humans, you created the internet and Youtube to be used on devices that you also inspired, and that anyone can use to accomplish that worship of you in Spirit and Truth because you are seeking for those kinds of worshippers /believers. That relationship for me is priceless.

I can agree with Solomon that I need more wisdom than I need money. Thank you for the Wisdom. I give all the glory and honor due my savior, your son, as the Holy Ghost In me, keeps me rejoicing always and again I say; I rejoice.

As if that wasn't enough, you inspired men like King James, Alexander Scourby, Fred Hammond, Pastor John P. Kee, and other inspirational artists who released sounds that fortify those who desire to worship you in their Secret Closet experiences in Spirit and Truth. Their songs and messages give us the words as proclaimed by Christ from the Holy Bible that is all free on the internet. Also known as Your super highway to communicate with Your Flock.

Free to all! A worship taking place in our **S**ecret **C**loset day and night.

You gave us Wisdom at the beginning, and equipped us with a force-and-power of instructions of truth-and-righteousness. You put, by the Holy Ghost, this power within every heart that seeks first the kingdom of God and all His righteousness. We ask and we receive, we seek and we find, we knock and doors open unto us, proving that the wise will hear Wisdom (Her) instructions and increase their learning.

Fools who hate knowledge will be sent into the pit prepared for the devil, and demons, who wail and gnash their teeth. We note that it's not your will that any should perish. All just have to look to Jesus to live, "Verily, verily I say to you if a man/woman keeps my sayings, he shall never see death." Even before the first death, your word showed that if men were to flourish on Earth, they would need the Wisdom from above. (John 8:51)

When we erred, you sent your Son, Jesus to die, as payment of the ransom required at the Garden's scene. Now we can partake of the Tree of Life, the Bread that came down from heaven, so that we may live freely throughout eternity. "Ye shall

Conclusion

know the truth, and the truth shall make you free." John 8:32. Truth has made us free, and now we live the abundant life.

"But as many as received him, to them gave he power to become the sons of God, even to them that believe in his name:" John 1:12. So, all believers can access eternal life freely because Jesus has paid the price; the only things they need to do is keep His word, and produce good fruits from their work and labor of love. We must remember the burial of the one talent-servant who was cast out. Wisdom taught us that this outcast suffered Eternal Death.

Jesus stopped the hemorrhaging of wickedness and permanent separation from your love and presence. The Law of the Spirit of life in Christ Jesus has made countless people free from the Law of Sin and Death.

He subdued the enemy; He conquered death, hell, and the grave for all that will call upon His Holy name. Jesus was re-Glorified with the Glory He had from the beginning. He has said that All Power in heaven and earth is now His, and His enemy is His footstool; He is above His fellow(s) while sitting at the right hand of Power.

I must lift Him up as the serpent in the wilderness of Moses' day in every way; in words, songs, books, the internet, social media, and testimony. Which will result in the drawing of men to His saving power.

Help me, Father, through revelations to be disciplined, patient, and grateful for your mercy and kindness toward humankind. Allow us to build a team worthy of your Honor and Glory as we continue to hear Wisdom Speak!

DONATE TO FREE BOOK CAMPAIGN

Hello to my loyal readers I am the Executive Director of

The 24 Minute Ministry, Inc

A Non-profit 501c3 Organization, I serve the public as a Chauffeur, Taxi, and other Tnc modes of Transportation.

As I work with Students at various Universities in Texas

My goal is to distribute this book to any student who will accept it without cost to them.

You can help with a small tax deductible donation to this

The 24 Minute Ministry, Inc™

Send your donations to:

The 24 Minute Ministry, Inc

PO BOX 152546

AUSTIN, TEXAS 78718

Email: Johnnie@The24MinuteMinistryInc.com

Visit our Website: www.MyNumberedDays.com ®

Phone: 888-858-3297 or 512-552-8688

Your contributions will support our Free Book campaign.

Conclusion

"I must work the work of Him that sent me the night cometh when no man can work"

--JESUS

www.ingramcontent.com/pod-product-compliance
Lightning Source LLC
Chambersburg PA
CBHW071459070526
44578CB00001B/390